A Lament of the Heart

A Lament of the Heart

The Torturous Chronicle of a Soul

Élyas Rivermark

To request permissions, contact the author at
e.rivermark.44@gmail.com

Hardcover: Coming Soon
Paperback: 979-8-9888143-0-6
Audiobook: Coming Soon
Ebook: 979-8-9888143-2-0

First Paperback Edition August 2023

Cover art by Galgan Design
Instagram: @galgan_design

For You who needs it most…

Table of Contents

In the Beginning...Walks in the Dark

Dearest Beloved,

In the spring of my first year at university, on returning from holiday, I experienced a number of days that ended in severe bouts of crushing loneliness. This was not because of your absence, nor the fact that I had left my family after a limited time at home; rather, the crushing weight of pure solitude rested on my shoulders. The dormitory in which I stayed was all but empty and the three roommates with whom I shared a suite were still at home. Three nights I spent alone, lost in my own thoughts and drowning in loneliness. I would forget about you and everyone else during the day while I was at work, your spirit instead lingering in the dark recesses of my mind, waiting to emerge at night when I was alone.

Those three nights spent alone in silence were broken by the routine of making supper for myself in the quiet kitchen as the murmurs of cliché love songs droned on through a little black speaker. I could tell you that I was sane during these times of cooking; cooking has of course always been a time where I can really let go of myself and be free. This, however, was not the case, instead I barely listened to the music as the words of the songs ghosted through my head, their meaning holding no sway in my life anymore. Looking back on those nights in the kitchen, I didn't know it, but I had fallen into an intense depression. Not in any kind of medical way, it was not caused by any kind of abuse. It was rather the hole that was slowly growing in my heart. There was a need that had never been truly filled as I had wanted it to be. In that kitchen, I was a puppet, its strings cut, sagging into itself as it looked for a purpose. The kitchen could not provide what I needed to hear, nor could any person in the dormitory, for there was no one in the building who could hear my internal cries for love and fellowship.

The kitchen could not provide what I needed during those nights, I thought perhaps that my old friend could. The old friend that brought me through so much heartbreak and sadness that I could not help but turn to him. It was not a person, nor any kind of drug or alcohol. It was the genre of romance films. Being able to see someone in a state of perfect love - however fake - usually pulled me out of any kind of love based stupor. I spent about two hours of that first night back at the dormitory watching one of those romantic comedy films, hoping that it might get me out of the hole I had created for myself. To my devastating surprise, my old friend could do nothing for me. I spent about two hours lying on a couch, falling faster and faster in an ever growing hole of unyielding sadness. I watched as the fantasy unfolded before me and the characters achieved more in the span of a few months than I could ever dream of grasping in years of failure. The effects of the bombardment of false love penetrated deeper into my heart and I could barely keep my wits about me. The old friend that I put so much of my heart and soul into began to rip the emotions from within me. The depressed state that already held sway over me made sure of that fact. I loved these films and rather than pull me out of the sorry state that gripped my life, it showed me love that I seemed to never be able to attain for myself as hard as I tried to do so.

I must admit that once the film was over, it was difficult to pull myself off of the couch and continue on with my usual nightly routine. I managed to drag myself to the washroom and get into the shower. The shower, in my mind, was a place of refuge and solitude. It was in this situation that I could be alone with my thoughts. On that night, the place of safety became instead the place of crushing weight and helplessness. It seemed that no matter where I went or what I turned to, a constant shadow continued to press against me. I could no longer bear it. I escaped that watery cell and rushed to a place that always promised comfort and safety. Sleep evaded me and I sank further.

It is at this point that there is only one sensible thing to do, and so, with incredible reluctance, I dressed in warm clothes and ventured out into the crisp night air. Intent on fixing my deflated state of being, I began to pray. It was not my usual prayer, asking God for protection or for guidance, but rather it was an earnest prayer for you, my heart of hearts.

As I look to the sky full of stars,
A sea of lights twinkling in the night
Every one, a soul with a name.
He called each to its place long ago.
Images of men and beasts dancing in black
In that sky lives so many,
So why must I feel so alone?

This world is filled too,
Souls living and breathing,
Each harbouring their own fears and doubts.
I can see every one.
Suffering or rejoicing...I feel it too.
I would offer my heart to each
Just to keep them all shining.
Indeed my chest is already empty
Pieces of my heart reside elsewhere.
Only a syphon remains.
For whatever love is given to me
Is given to another that needs it more.
They come and go
Taking their share
Never placing a piece back in my chest.
I trust enough to love without restraint
Yet I never receive true love in return.
Only the curse of solitude...
Feeling my heart burn.

Élyas Rivermark

I reach out my hand in faith
Some hold it but briefly
Others return it…bleeding
Why must it hurt this way?

God
Free me from this pain
Fill my chest with pieces of your heart,
May I give them away instead of my own?
I would reach out my hand
I pray that you would put out yours
Heal my wounds.
I do not want my heart to bleed
But I will never stop loving
So please…
Wrap your arms around me
Guard my heart against those that wish to break it.
If it must be broken
Please
Repair it with veins of gold.

Forgive me for this lament.
I am a broken man .
My pieces lie scattered,
Beaten and bloody,
Slowly being reduced to ash.
In my world of grey
You are my light and my joy.
Let me live for you
Show me your path
For I cannot see it,
I yield it all to you
For I cannot walk this life alone.

… What follows is a story of love gained and lost, laments from the depths of my heart, to little poems that came upon me as I walked. All are a part of my soul and so they have been mostly unedited. Once my pencil finished a line, that line was seldom touched again. Some of the poems that follow, I am very proud of and wish they would speak to you as they have to me. Some have come out of elation and a love so deep that I feared it may have swallowed me. Others come from a state so destitute that the raw emotion was too much for my heart to handle at the time.

At the end of my life, I will look back on each and every one of these poems and be amazed at the path that I have taken. I have loved deeply and I have wept in a sorrow so strong. Yet every moment I lived for God and I lived for you. My beloved you are the reason I speak these words, you are the reason I am who I am.

I will always be…

The Knight of Your Heart,

Élyas

Élyas Rivermark

If I Die

My life has never been my own
I feel I am running out of time
Every day is a blessing.
No, I am not dying
Not yet,
Though I may be taken early
It is not something I chose
Yet I feel it in my heart
I may not live a full life.

Do not be afraid my dear
I do not fear death.
I will return to my Father
Dancing up those steps so quickly
Strings tugging at my heart
I would freely leave this life.

If I die
Do not shed a tear for me.
I shall be with you always
Watching over you.
On wings of light I will fly
Battling as I always have
Killing the rot on your heart
Fighting your demons.

I know not where you are.
If I am taken from this world
I pray you did not love me.
For *if I die*
I could not bear your sorrow

Nor a little one left behind.
So I will continue this life alone
Never so selfish to fall for you.
For I can only give a little time
Until my death.
Short as a life can be
I still love you.

I do not want to die
I want to live forever with you.
A prayer always on my lips
Asking Him to keep me here
I may see those moments…
A ring
A child
And your smile.
Lord let me live long
Wither away slowly
Smile widening by the day.

If I die
Let it be before I fall
For I could not bear it
To see your tears once I am gone
Though I will always love you
I pray you do not fall for me.
For even though I love you
I want your heart to remain whole.
So let me not be torn from this world.

I love my life
I do not wish to take it.
But I have felt it
The inkling of a prophecy on my heart.

Élyas Rivermark

I am to leave this life
So much time left to live.
Be this a fine confession
To say that I have lived this life
Loving those that need it
Being loved in return.
I am happy with this short life
So, *if I die*
Know that I leave this world a happy man.

To have loved you so fully
Though you did not love me
I would rather have that
Than to see you alone
Wishing I was still there
Not taken by accident
By disease or evil.

If you love me
Know that I will give my life
Every moment, to your heart.
And *if I die*
Do not be angry.
I lived as I ought
My candle burned through.
It burned for you
For my family
Everyone around me.

I gave all I could give
So
If I die
I am finished
My task here is done.

To love you with everything
May it be my only charge.
For when I am gone
I pray I opened your heart
Take me now.
If I die
I shall not be afraid…

Élyas Rivermark

That Gaze of Perfect Love

Oh that gaze of love
That flutters as silent as a dove.
Into the eyes and mind of a man
As he gazes upon his woman without ban
It is but so subtle
That she could not manage a rebuttal.

Oh that gaze of love
Which hides from confrontation.
Only to appear when she has no inclination
Of the devout loyalty of her man.

Oh that gaze of love
Hoping to remain hidden
Until it knows it is not forbidden.
It is then that the man may not avert his gaze
But charge into the fray unfazed

Oh that gaze of perfect love
That only comes unbidden
Until she coaxes it to remain unhidden.

Kiss Like the Rain

Feel that gentle and cool caress part your lips
Experience the embrace as all your worries melt away
A kiss is only a kiss
But with love?
We *kiss like the rain.*

Élyas Rivermark

Love's Leave-Taking

I wish that things could have been different
To speak of love as if she is here
A love between friends
That is all it ever was.
An appreciation of things shared
She could not thrive within our hearts.

Love cannot survive on force of will alone
Even less so on the will of a broken heart.
The love I lead is a one-way street
It bears the curse of friendship
Existing in a land where love does not come for it.

Love has not deserted me.
I feel it in my heart every day.
But from romance I'm afraid
I can find no return

With sorrow I must accept
Love's Leave-Taking.

Slow Dances in the Dark

You were in a blue dress
One that matched the mood of my heart.
But that smile
It echoed like laughter in the rain
So gentle, but it struck me with light.
A hole of black my chest had once been
Now it shines like the moon.
I pull you close.
I take your gentle hand.
I wrap my life around you.
It is right that I should do so.
Step with me, I will guide you along the way
Listen to the music of my heart
And do more than just stay.
I will hold you until my arms give out
And my legs cannot stand
I will hold you forever
As we *slow dance in the dark.*

Élyas Rivermark

Dancing in the Dark

There were long walks in the dark
My heart weeping, taken by the king of the night
But my feet, moving forward, aided by the spectres of the light
My heart is broken, lying useless as the pieces turn to dust.

They rise again, built by your soft hand
Caressing each piece
My angel of a girl.
Come again and take my heart away
Press your heart to mine and with the music sway.
Come with me into the night
There will be long walks in the dark.

She used to walk with me...
Warm nights, cold nights, happy as can be
She left without a word, she left without a trace
Smashed my heart into pieces
Come please, say it to my face.
I gave her more than I could give
And yet, she stole the only thing that made me live
Give back my heart once more
I'll place it in the hands of someone worth dying for.
Give me someone who meets the mark and enjoys
Long walks...*Dancing in the dark.*

You picked me up, gave me life
Breathed light into me, gave me a spark.
When your hand touched mine
My soul breathed its first, free of strife.
When your lips touched mine
Their light cast away the long dark.
Let me gather you into my arms
Never let go...
Show me your eyes, the ones so bright
And let me show you my love
Evermore into the night.

I will go through hell and back
If only to see your face again
But follow me
We'll go

Running into the dark.

Élyas Rivermark

Torn

To love is to choose.
To choose is to break.
Making that break does more to me
Than I have the strength to endure
I love her
But to her I give my love also.

To each I give my love
Expecting nothing in return.
Where will God take me?
To her I could go
But to her I would go also…

Torn is my heart between two angels.
They do not pull themselves
Yet my heart goes to both
A string attached to both ends.
Torn am I between love and love.
Neither reciprocal and yet…
I love with everything I have.
God, fix this tear
Push me towards my angel
Torn between them I will be forever
Until you send her to me.

Makes Me Weak

Love is weakness
Love is strength
Your love *makes me weak*
I see your smile, the glint in your eyes
I feel my legs begin to shake
My heartbeat stops.
A moment of ecstasy enters my mind
As I begin to fall
Free to fall, weightless into your arms.

A moment of weakness,
But a moment of rejoice
Feeling weakness does not frighten me
Instead, I use that weakness
To cleave closer to you.
My love for you rages in my heart.
That alone makes me strong;
I think of you every waking moment.

Those moments *make me weak*
But I will rejoice in my weakness.

Élyas Rivermark

Heart of Stone

Cold…
Cold is my heart
My *heart of stone*, lying in the dark
Festering in the damp recesses of my chest.
It may not soften
The walls are too thick.

I have built these walls
Yet you broke them down
With your smile and your lips, you tore them down.
I allowed you to warm my heart,
That warmth was too brief
For you tore my heart to pieces.

Now I must rebuild these walls of stone
Thicker and thicker than before.
Let me build my walls.
To *a heart of stone* I must return,
Cold and hard to the world,
It keeps the pain away
In stone, I will endure.

A Windy Evening

A windy evening…
As the wind kissed the tops of the trees
I found myself walking down a path.
A past quite forgotten
Reared its head in my mind like a dream.
Coaxing my spirit to remember
An evening that had long grown dark.

She had worn a pale lavender dress
Her smile shone brighter than any star
And in that moment I cared not
I did not care for the wind that whipped
It flowed…two sprites tangled in a dance
It passed through me, biting and cold.

To the girl in the lavender dress
It only caressed
It embraced her pale form
She laughed
A spirit in her own right.
A spirit who made her home in the deep recesses of my heart.

On *that windy evening*
I found the woman destined to have my love forever
That fateful night, a spirit wrapped in lavender
Danced with the wind.
Swirling and curling down that beautiful path
I fell in love, my soul entranced by the fey spirit before me.

Élyas Rivermark

She continued, laughing and smiling down that path
Her steps muffled by the soft dirt
It caressed her feet clad in black.
Those steps began to strike stone
Its echo travelling to no-one's ear but mine
Onto a cobblestone street her steps took her
Her laugh never ceasing.

I watched this spirit in the night
Awe in my eyes.
She shone like the moon
So bright, yet so tranquil
Brighter and brighter still.

As this memory bears down upon me,
I wish I could have changed it
Her laugh still rings in my ear
A smile so bright it could have killed me.
She looked back at me as she entered that street
Begging to be swept up in my arms.

As I walked that path,
The lavender dress seemed to glow
Wind tugging at the fringes
So bright she became..
But it was too late.

A creation of man took her from me
What was once lavender
Stained with streams of red.
A laugh so musical
Had gone silent.
Full of poison a man had become
Moving too fast down that cobblestone street

A Lament of the Heart

She did not have the chance to turn
Nor I to save my love.
Taken from me, my soul was no more
It fades to memory, only to return with the wind.

Élyas Rivermark

Scents of Comfort

We find comfort in song
In film
In the touch of our other half
To smell?
That is a whole other beast
The cologne of my father
The embrace of my mother
These bring back memories of days long past.
The dirt of a diamond
A breeze carrying the moisture of the first spring rain
For us, smell can be everything
Even the unknown can bring back memories.

In the span of but a moment
A flood of memories may flow past
They carry neither joy nor dread
Just a sense of peace.
Days go by
Moments filled with stories
Told by *scents of comfort.*

A Hug

There are no words to describe what it truly feels like
To run to someone, their heart pressed firmly onto yours…
Their hand lightly resting on the small of your back
That gentle touch becomes fierce
When they begin to fall
But *a hug* holds you up.

A hug from a friend promises love.
A hug from a mother does the same.
A hug from a father promises protection.
From a sibling?
Empathy, and a promise that they understand.
A hug ensures love
Before anything else
You may know that someone will always love you.

Élyas Rivermark

It Was to Be Us

For many years I prayed to find you
A woman to match
A woman for whom I could live
Love is said to be split in half
That is a lie…
For you I could be whole
For me I pray you could do the same.

It was to be us
Two souls joined against this world
Dancing in the kitchen
Small talks in bed
Long walks through the park
I could have been a fool for you
It was to be us.
Two fools experiencing life
One day at a time.

It will be us, when I finally find you
It will be us, when you find me
It was to be us
It was to be us.

You are the Reason

My love,
You wonder why I get up in the morning
It is not to work
'Tis but a passing thing, an inconvenience
A means by which I can provide.
It is not to drink my coffee
It is not to cook breakfast
You are the reason
Through you I have the strength to rise.
My love
Why do I rush home every day?
It is not for the love of the screen
Nor the comfort of the couch.
Just to see that smile
Excitement as you talk about the day.
You are the reason
Through you I have the haste to return
Into your arms I will always fall
I have a reason to love
A reason to pray.
A reason to live.

You are the reason.

A Vault

A Vault,
A heart of stone
That name no longer fits
For my heart is so soft
With it I cannot live.
A hard heart may be cracked
A soft one will bleed.
So lock it up
With walls of iron protect it
Keep me from this incessant pain!

Did You Know it Was You

You ask whom do I love
I say an angel sent from Heaven.
You ask what do I see
I say the radiance of a gorgeous smile.
You ask when will I love
I say as soon as she knows.
You ask where I find her
I say in the space of a moment.
You ask why do I live
I say for the kisses like rain.
You ask how do I know
I say the moment she laughed.

Who is this woman I speak of?
She is the one to whom my stone heart belongs
Her hands warm my soul
Her eyes pierce my heart
Her smiles live in my mind
Her touch kills me
Into her arms I will fall
She never let go
Brought me from darkness into light.
Did you know it was you?

Élyas Rivermark

She Had a Nose Ring

What do the jewels mean?
Those that adorn your face
The diamonds in your ears
They are elegance
Hoops share that meaning
Rings, many of them, for whom?
A wave for those sandy beaches
Plain bands to fill the void
A small gem containing a promise.

Those things that pierce your body
They pale beside the necklace that you wear
Except for one.
A thin band that pierces your nose.
Its meaning is ten-fold.
What brought you to the state?
A dark past
A state of rebellion
Or just the changes of the world?
Not everyone can wear one, it is a rule.
One to which you are an exception
For that simple band
Brings your comfort to my heart.

We Are All the Protagonist

Who are you?
You who shakes with the weight of yourself
God does not punish you for your choices
Only tests them
He tests you, an author discovering your story
Do not dismay
This part of your tale does not end here.

You are not faceless.
You have power.
Take life one day into the next
Let your heart lead you.
Your mind keep you safe
Control is given to you
Take it and let your soul sing.
A side character in another's story
Do not mistake theirs for your own.

We are all the Protagonist
Discovering our own journey
Take heart in that
Do not be dismayed.

Élyas Rivermark

Finally...A Happy Song

Life takes us to dark places
Though it takes less to smile
We find ourselves straining to frown
Why must we work so hard
To find ourselves at the end of our soul?

To be joyful
Where are the times filled with laughter
We can conjure poison in our past
But to find light?
That is a rare gift.

When I am with you
I can hear it.
I can see the song of our life being written
For me, you burn the darkness away
Your warmth spreading
A sun, rising into my life
Unto you I pour my love.
For you my heart sings
Finally... A happy song

A Heart That Beats For You

A heart that beats slowly
Drums echoing in my chest
Every beat is so strong.

You lie your head upon my chest
What do you hear?
I have heard:
"You sound as if you are dead"
"Do I not excite you? It ought to be racing"
"Perhaps I am hurting you"

I do not know why I beat so slow and strong
Perhaps my heart is always at peace.
A heart that beats with every breath you take
Stopping only when you have your last.
It beats with you.

I lay you down
Rest my ear on your breast
Like the fluttering of wings
Your heart races under the heaving of your chest
Why does it stutter so?

You are the soul of my soul
The heart of my heart.
I will breathe everything I have into loving you
Every thump within me
I hope it echoes in you
I wish your heartbeat would not flutter
But resound and fill your chest.

Élyas Rivermark

I know your heart
I understand it as my own
I would give it to you
Please take it from me.

You ask where I have gone.
I return to those that gave me my heart
It was so slow and strong
Keeping me with you
So that it may be given to you
I gave you my heart and soul
Please keep them near to your own
Beating again like a drum.
It is the only way to keep you living.

My heart now beats for you.

It Was But a Dream

What is a dream?
A fragmented memory of a future not yet reachable
A tale so fantastic your mind cannot fathom its depths.
Fears made real
Monstrosities brought to life
Each feeding off the corners of your imagination.

Lying in bed at night
I wonder
Wonder what stories will be told
Memories retold
Fears realised
Or the black abyss takes me until my rude awakening.

Before slipping into a deep slumber
You appear before my eyes.
I recall things about you
Things so small but significant.
The way you raise your brow
How your hair falls
Waves of gold caressing your face
Shining out of the dark
Your eyes like sapphire
A dress to match
Branded onto my heart unyielding.

You shine before me
Yet I cannot touch you
The feeling of your kiss upon my lips
Your fingers brushing against my cheek
The comfort of your presence

Élyas Rivermark

They are unknown to me.
I have felt your embrace
I have heard the beauty of your laugh
The intensity of your gaze
The friendship that we carry.

But I have not felt your love truly
To know the love of others is not strange.
In dreams
Therein I can create something
The true meaning of your love escapes me
But through others
My dreams can produce a ghost.
A shadow of the possible love you carry
The kiss is not yours
The touch is by a different hand.

I have never felt your heart
Blossoming underneath my touch
O how I wish I could hold you
I will hold you forever.
My soul is yours
Of this I am certain.
I would keep nothing from you
I care nothing for physicality
Only to feel your presence
But alas
It was but a dream
Nothing more …

Your Name

For fear of making my emotions known
Or the desire to protect you from inquiry
Revealing *your name* will never occur.

Kill me with the joy you bring to my heart
Already I can be nothing but your own
Would you take me as I am?
Every part of me is yours to hold
Let not *your name* escape my lips
If only I could shout it to Heaven
Night could not take me.

With you I could escape the bonds of shadow
A prayer of *your name* sets me free
Heavenly light shines through you
Show me the way into life
Hearts, like ours, can only survive as one.

Élyas Rivermark

She Doesn't Even Know

Have you known?
The bliss that comes with being joyful
Finding all that you need in them?

I have found it.
When I see her face
My heart blazes anew
Raging to see her smile that kills me.
She can bake.
What I would give to taste that love
To embrace her in the kitchen
And be surrounded by the comfort of her.

She can sing.
I wonder to whom she writes
To her I spill my soul
My hand moving on its own.
Who moves her hand?
My heart hopes that one day it will be me
Perhaps she already sings to me
In her heart she knows of my love
I hope that God has put me there.

But in her mind she is alone
She sings out into the abyss
Calling up memories that are not there.
I am here.
I am listening.
An angel's voice escapes her lips
Heaven's gift flows through her

And yet,
She doesn't even know.
Small memories we have shared
They meant the world to me
Every second resounding in my mind
Every smile engraved upon me
How do I tell her?
She doesn't even know
What should I say?
She must know that I love her
But I would die
If I scared her away.

Élyas Rivermark

Something Else Begins

Since the age of nine
I have wanted nothing more
But to be married and have children of my own
Throughout life I showed this to anyone that would listen.

To every girl that I ever gave my heart to
I gave them every piece of me
Still
I would give up my life for them
I would cease my breath
To save any life.
Changing this quality is not possible
For the fear of being helpless
Remains too strong in my chest
Every beat of the heart
I would give to those I love.

For all my life
Convinced I was only hers
Realisation struck one lonely night.

Romance has always moved me
God has spoken to me through film.
One night, He spoke to me
Told me that I ought to reach
Reach for those in my heart
For my life is short
I love you.
It takes but a breath
I thought that I ought to save it
Save those "I love yous" for her.

My heart is much too big for that
To my family,
I love you.
My best man
You, to whom I promised my heart
Friends divided by distance.
Little more than strangers.
To all,
You have my heart.

After that night
One guided not by me
Whatever it was
Why it happened
I know not.

Changed by your love
Somehow, my heart opened.
You allowed it to be filled
Once more filled to the brim.
God you work through me
Speak love to those that need it
Through me
Let your love provide a home
A hand to hold
A hug to give
Anywhere that I'll ever go.

My search for true love never ends
But that night
This night
Something else begins.

Élyas Rivermark

Fellowship

Sprinting through life
We see those with whom we compete
Pushing ever forward
Hoping that we might cross that line.

Do you see them?
There is love spilling over you
We fought by ourselves, never alone.
To the right
A smile and a wink as they push past
Not competing
But pushing to be better
To the left
Shouts pound at your ears
Giving support and love with every step.

Life is not a game to be won.
Muster your army
Attack quickly
Engage in diplomacy
These are all part of the war of life.

There is no right way
We live for life's sake
Do not live to gloat
There is love all around you
You need only reach out.

A Lament of the Heart

We fight life
Each engaging in a different battle
But alone
Never will we be on our own.

Find love, for it does not hide
It comes in your hour of need
Charging over the hill
The sound of trumpets heavy
The beat of shouts strong
A wave of those fighting for you
Ever present.

On the ground
Beaten and bloody
Lying in struggle
Looking to escape
Hands reach down
Grasping your life
Never will you be a burden.
There are many who love you
One to bring you in
Two who live for you
One to make you laugh
One who loved you, but no more
Some far away, ever vigilant.

Élyas Rivermark

Every soul among them
A brother
A sister
We live for eachother.
Pouring out our love every day
Becoming a rock on which to stand
A shoulder to cry on
A secret keeper
Those that push us to the limit.

Everyday we live in the light of one another
A *fellowship* of friends
One that could never be torn
By distance nor time
It will always remain strong.

Never a Good "Bye"

It is never enough, to say hello
For when we say that fateful word
There is sure to be a goodbye.
I am loathe to say farewell
For it could end in forever
So, my darling
Let me instead…

Hold you in my arms
Allow me to rest my eyes upon you
Your fingers run through my hair
The gentle breeze of your breath upon my face
As I look upon you
Painting a memory until next we meet
Every moment
Every smile
Branded upon me.

I will not allow you to say goodbye
For fear that it may be the last
Do not say it
For hope, say not a farewell.
In its place
Give me your love only
Grant me one more kiss upon my brow
And blink those oceans of blue
I could not forget your face
Nor the touch of your hand.

Élyas Rivermark

Let not farewell escape your lips
For if I could travel back
I would steal it before it came
I cannot bear to say goodbye.
Only to have you here
My forever I will give to you
If only to never hear you utter those words.
I would only hear goodnight
For that ushers in a good morning.
But a farewell is never good
Full of sadness
Full of longing
Please never part from me.

For there is *Never a good "bye"*

I Would Give Up

In love we all partake in acts of insanity
There has never been any act too extreme in your name
You are my dream
For you *I would give up* everything
My world, gone dark if not for you.

I would give up my eyes
If it meant hearing your voice.
My ears would I give also
To see your beautiful face.
My arms,
So that I may sprint to your side
My legs,
Gone, letting me feel the touch of your hand.

I would give up my sanity
Just to hear you sing.
For when you sing
It brings light into my darkness
Life into my soul.
When you sing,
I know that the angels sing with you
So it matters not, where my mind is
Perhaps falling into darkness
But with your voice I know to fly.
Your words lift me up
Pulling me from any abyss.

Élyas Rivermark

I would give up my life
If it meant that you could continue.
My life be forfeit
Only to hear you laugh one more time.
Beauty exists in you
My eyes drink it in
Only to avert my gaze
When you look back at me
Perhaps I may grow stronger
Look back at you with love.
For love you I must
Even if it costs me my life.

There is but one thing
One I could not release
For it is not mine to give.
My soul I would not give up
The Lord keeps it in his company
If he so chooses
He may give it to you
I urge him to do so
If you would only accept it.

If you refuse
I could not be angry
For as my own, your soul is God's to give.
He may not give it to me
So even after all of this…

I would give up.

She's Beautiful

They say she blazes like the sun
I say she shines like the moon
Of all the stars in the sky
She is the only thing.
With eyes like emeralds
Hair like harvest wheat
I cannot divert my eyes
She may not be Aphrodite
But to me?

She's Beautiful

Élyas Rivermark

The Gravity of Love

Falling in love is the most dangerous thing.
There is no sense to it
Yet we leap without sense.
Falling.
Hoping they might reach out.

When we take that fateful leap
We understand fully *the gravity of love*
It cares not on whom it pulls
Plucking our heartstrings…
It urges us to the edge.
We may look at the abyss before us
Full of life or sorrow
Its forces yearn for our presence
Would you leap with me?

Do not be afraid.
For in life we would smile
And in sorrow we would weep.
With you I do not fear love
I would jump freely.
My heartstrings pull taut
The force before me grasps at my feet.
I would go forward
Would you leap with me?

A Lament of the Heart

My love,
I know not what the abyss holds
Life is never that clear
Our path is never our own
Two may become one
A third may carry us both
His footprints stretching out before us
In faith we might walk
Following Him through the void
Trusting Him with a soft landing.

The gravity of love tears me down
With you I could bear its weight
Please trust in me
Take my hand
And we will take His
Into the future of the unknown
Into love.
We must leap.

To the edge of the abyss
The gravity of love pulling harder.
Its ache ever so strong in my chest
Two hearts together on the edge
A spirit hanging above
The unknown stretched beneath.

I turn to look upon you once more
Remembering every detail.
I can see the joy in your eyes
Feel the burning of your heart.
You look back at me with a smile
In it I find my strength
You say you will try.

Élyas Rivermark

I am laid bare.
With my back to the abyss
I see you.
And I no longer fear the dark.
With your hand in mine
I close my eyes.
The darkness below my feet does not frighten me
One last look into your eyes
My hand slips from yours.

I am falling.

Forgive Me My Mistakes

Dearest Beloved,

I ask at this moment for your forgiveness, I have made so many mistakes. Now, of course, I know that my condition is that of human nature, but regardless, I ask from the depths of my heart, would you forgive me?

As I look back at the journal of my life, there are too many instances in which I have placed your image on those that would not hold it. Through no fault of their own, they were simply, not you. In those moments I am reminded of a saying that to this day, I struggle to believe: "You will know that you have met the 'one' when loving is as easy as breathing." In all honesty, I had believed that this statement was totally and utterly false. Up until this very moment, as I am writing this letter, I had believed that love was work. I believed that if I had just tried hard enough, I had shown enough love to someone, it would eventually come back to me. Now I know that the saying is true. I have seen it played out time and time again by others in my life. So, I am waiting until that day comes for me. I am reminded of a letter that I had once written almost five years ago about someone I had thought that I truly loved after so much heartbreak.

...

Feelings are such a fickle thing in this short life that we live, how do we best describe what they are used for? Let me first start with love, I wonder how best to describe something I have never truly felt. Am I now beginning to see a faint glimmer of it? What do I feel?

I know that I feel giddy when I call her and hear her voice and I am anticipating that time throughout the day (every moment she seems to creep into the forefront of my mind) is that love, or is it interest that stems from distance? I hope not, because with every new detail of her character, I fall more and more into a hole that seems to be getting deeper. No... falling is perhaps not the right word. I am reminded of a lecture where a professor describes it as rising into love. It began with no real expectations, but if marriage is my end goal, then I am rising closer to that first step of love.

They say that love is blind, I say that the love that is blind is not true love. Finding faults in someone but loving them anyway is the true measure of love. She smiles a little too much with her teeth sometimes and when she puts her hair into a ponytail, it does not look the best, but then again, there are things that I do that do not look good either. I have doubts that stem from the belief that I could find someone straight out of a magazine, but how could I say something so naive? Beauty in magazines is fake, but she is a woman of God, she loves old music and movies, how much more could I truly ask for? I know that she has prayed for a man to come along as I have often prayed for a woman. Is this an answer to my prayers?

By the sudden quelling of my heart and the clarity in my mind, I believe that this is your answer. From this moment forward, I will do everything in my power to fight for her. I want to become the Knight of her Heart, whatever that may take. I stand by what I say, she is as beautiful as the sunrise and shines into my mind with the power of an angel...

I enjoy reflecting on these letters that I have written, because in that moment, I had believed that I was truly in love. I had dived headfirst with no regard for my own heart. I want you to understand that this is how my love works. I have never, and will never hold back my love from you. It will start out small and timid, like the flame of a match it provides just a small amount of light. Over time it will grow into an inferno, a love so strong that it will consume all of me. Our love will truly be like breathing. I believe that on the day that I meet you, I know that all these efforts will not be in vain. The women I have loved before were indeed loved. Unfortunately my style of love was not for them. I love so much and so fiercely, often it frightens people away.

Truly, there is a saying that I do not find valid: "You will find your true love when you finally stop looking." I trust in the fact that one day I will find you, but how could I find you if neither you nor I are searching? How many times have I passed you by? How many times have we crossed paths but our eyes are blind to each other?

I know the plan for my life, if I was to meet you then, I am sure that I would have failed you as I had so many before. My life keeps changing, I am growing evermore by the year, so I know that when I meet you, I will be the best I can be for you.

I am trying to not torture myself with these musings, I know that when I meet you I will be so easily happy, so in love and so enamoured by you. Often, I have pleaded for you, not only for someone to love, but someone who I can truly share my life with. There is so much I want to tell you and to tell all of those that have changed my life, but I have a feeling my time to do so is running out.

The Knight of Your Heart,

Élyas

Élyas Rivermark

Ideal Yet Real

It begins, a mirror of every other.
A gaze, a touch, a word
It matters not.
A spark flickers, I coax it forth
Bring life to a feeling deep inside
Let it rage beneath the surface.
Use it to fuel my own passion.

Fighting the storm inside is folly
Instead, surrender to the heart
Let it guide the soul
But do not fall into a dream
Have faith, but do not submit to a shadow
Surrender your own heart
Fight for theirs
Never cease your love.
Let it never come from a mirage
Love them like the movies
Yet never stray from reality.

Indeed
Look to the little moments
Let them take your breath away.
Savour them
And rest in the eyes of the storm.
Let them shield you from evil.

Love can become something greater
Have hope for the greatest of all things.
Bring peace in the worst
There is beauty in reality.

Love has its big moments
When two may become one
Two becomes three and four
A surprise five
Followed by a hopeful six
The passage of time gives love strength.
Not without struggle
Growth instead comes with every moment
Even more special than the last.

Take comfort in the process
For it begins with a feeling.
Two strangers connected by a string
Moments pass through time
Those strangers become close
Two souls slowly connecting at the core.

Love is not perfect
Days go by, full of pain.
In them also, times of peace
Let yourself take those in
Focus not on the suffering.
For in love, it will be brief
In love, we are not alone
Challenges faced by one
Begin to find aid in another
Two cannot fail.

Élyas Rivermark

When I fall in love
Let it be forever
Let me strive for the ideal
I know perfection will never come
But I will aim so high
To the ends of the Earth
To the moon
I will reach until I fall.
My love,
Let me not fall
Unless it be in love with you
Let me fall into your arms
I would put my heart into your hands.
Could you put yours into mine?

Love is real.
True love is possible.
Understand that it will never be perfect
Yet with every breath
We grow one step closer
With every fight
We become one.
I would understand you
Give me your ideal
For true love never ceases reaching for that ideal.
We could settle in, reality is sweet
As long as it is with you.

Souls of Darkness

I have felt it
It has devoured my heart before.
Therefore, I have named its touch
Because for me it is an apocalypse.
Crushing weight heaped upon me
A growing fear that you have slipped
Slipped through my fingers.

My darling
I could never blame you
For there are thorns in my past
Removing them myself is impossible
I do not have the strength of will.
Walls have been built
When they are broken down
The dark thorn is exposed
But none have been removed
They fester in the dark
Gnawing at my mind day by day.

I despise this darkness of mine
I wish the thorns were never made.
But I cannot control others
Past loves have destroyed parts of me
Parts I strive to rebuild
I build them for you.
A thousand times I would build
A thousand times I would break
So that the last time I build
I build my life with you.

Élyas Rivermark

There is another in my life
He has healed me so much
I trust in His path.
For mine has only brought pain.
In the midst of the apocalypse
There may be peace.
In the darkness of my past
He showed me the light.
Some thorns have been removed
Some are left for you
So, in patience I must wait.

I know that you have thorns of your own
In every life there is pain
I believe I have the strength
Not for myself
But for you.
I would remove your thorns
I would bring joy to your sorrow
With you I am strong.
Let me in
I will open my heart to you
This is what love does
I will heal for you
Would you heal for me?

I know not yet who you are
Yet I know this in my heart
Today, we are apart.
One day could create a new start.
Two *souls of darkness*
Looking toward the light.

In Your Arms I Must Die

I do not fear death.
Would you believe I have felt its touch?
In my father's arms I had lain
Each breath comes only through pain
Yet I have no memory of that moment
Only the fear that it left behind.
I breathe now to feel connected
My soul feels empty without it.
Deeply do I breathe
To assure that I am living.
For some, it is but a passing thought
But for me?
Every breath brings every sensation
They are pain, and they are release
I cannot escape this fate.

I do not fear death
I fear when my breath will be taken.
Forgive me if at first I fear you
I do not often give my breath away
It is sacred to my own heart.
Forgive me.
For I will show you a fraud
A chest full of normal breaths
To keep you close
I cannot scare you away.

Élyas Rivermark

I do not fear death
Only my own revelation of breath
I would bring you close to my chest
I promise to hold you near.
But I will not breathe
I am terrified of what you might think.

So strong and deep they are
Like rushing wind through a storm.
Slowly
With each slow beat of my heart
I would breathe you in.

I do not fear death
Just let me breathe.
For if I am to leave this place
Be it alone
Stay and live your life
For in your arms I must die.

Right Here

You will not see
Every moment you sink faster
Every minute spent mourning the past.
I have seen what they did to you
The whole world is watching in scorn.
But me
I saw you.
I could see your heart
It shined so bright for me
Yet the world only saw its shell
A shell of your own creation.
I would not break it
I could not bear to have mine broken
A shell built to keep away the pain
To keep everyone close
To show them that you are okay.

Please give me your shell
For you will not need it
Show me the truth of your heart
I will not break it
I am *right here.*

Élyas Rivermark

A Life Worth Living

When the light of my heart begins to dim
I know that I am to start a new life
Without pain, without sorrow.
My soul is forever calm
To be with my Father in eternal bliss.

Until that day comes
Am I to suffer?
A lone lotus in the depths of a cave
The light of my heart blazes
It shows me the paths I might take
On which I know not where you will be.
The blossom of my soul lies beyond
A shadow hidden within the darkness
I can see your figure
Nothing more.

The light of my heart
It has shone brightly on the weeds
Flames of my love ever upon them
Into blossoms had I turned them
Pieces of me sinking deep within them.
Into beautiful flowers they sprouted
Yet not for me.
They remained weeds
Thorns that tore my love away
Leaving holes and scars.
Yet brighter still did I burn
Your image just out of reach
One of hope and love I could strive for.

A Lament of the Heart

In my delusions
I have forced your image on the weeds.
I call them weeds,
For weeds they are to me
But not to him or him
To others they are a saving grace.
To me?
They were the lies I told
Lies to make my heart feel whole
Lies that always broke me.
I am a mere shell
A shell of a man.
Cracks riddling the surface
Please come and save me.

My heart
It burns for your touch
It blazes for your love
I know you do not hide
You blaze for me as I yearn for you.
But alas, we are not ready.
The One in Heaven is waiting.
His plan is perfect
As our patience wears thin
His love grows stronger.
These cracks we bear
They are not in vain
I have gold, gold in my heart to fix it.
In yours I will find solace
Comfort will once again return to me.
Please come and save me.

Élyas Rivermark

Many years have I lived
The flame of my heart dwindling
Further and further still
Your shadow becomes unknown to me
I can no longer see your face
The weeds surround me.
Empty promises of love
Piercing my already broken heart
In my search for you
I have only found pain
I cannot hope to continue
Every step is agony.
The darkness presses in so strongly
A heart once so bright
Is losing its strength to burn.
The love I give is often not returned.
My family and my God
They keep my heart alight.
But these thorns, ever do they throb
Please come and save me.

In this small circle of light
I see new life
Those that were weeds
They have become so beautiful.
Each day happiness surrounds me
Behind me a path of green
A past of life, middling in the dark.

I do not regret my own life
These scars I bear, they are for you.
I do not ask to be fixed
Only that my beauty be found in my flaws
Pour gold into the cracks.

I will do the same for you
For we are broken together.
Please come and save me.

I have left my mark on many
A weed I am
A weed to those that did not need me.
Those that marked me and broke me
I have harmed them in return
I am not proud of this.
Nor do I wish it upon another
But to you I will not be a weed
Instead through me the world will know.
I have a profound ability to love.
I will love you with everything
But never be a burden.

I have struggled in this life of mine
But every pain filled step
Every moment of agony
They bring me closer to you.
God has carried me in moments I could not walk alone
He is my rock and my foundation.
But you,
You will have my breath.
A mortal life spent living with you.

Élyas Rivermark

These moments filled with joy,
Morning coffees
Warm nights in the winter
Sweaty days in the summer,
Every day…
Whether it be bright or gloomy
We shall burn together
No longer searching
Dwindling in the dark.
I am coming to you
With you I want so desperately to live,
A life worth living.

So Far Away

I understand the distance
Walking ever onward, you are there
You never leave my sight.
Step by laborious step
I inch ever closer to that beautiful embrace.
To see you walk down that aisle
I would give anything.
Yet that day does not come
It shies away from my sight
Hidden among the shadows of the future.

Why are you not with me?
I have been waiting
Waiting for that moment when I will know.
It will not come in a flash.
But after years I will see
You were made for me.
Am I not made for you?
Please tell me why
Why do you seem *so far away?*

Élyas Rivermark

How Do You Appear to Be

I have asked myself alone in the dark
How do you appear to be?
Often in a dream I have met you
For to you my heart has been given
Over and over I have pledged myself
But dreams matter not.
Where are you now?
Have I met you before?

In a coffee shop I have seen you
Under the fiery canopy of autumn
The peaceful white of winter
A flower you will ever be in spring.
There is nothing more beautiful
Nothing in this world worth more
More than the beauty within you.

I am prepared to meet you
I have changed everything I am.
At least
I have become everything I want.
Though I will always continue to grow.

A Lament of the Heart

How do you appear to be?
Are you broken inside?
I think perhaps you could be with them
The other that has your heart
I pray they do not break it.
If they do, know that my heart is big enough
Big enough to love for you and for me.
I have loved and died enough
Release me from this cycle.
I am finished.
I do not want to start over again.

With you?
I would start over a hundred times
No
Every moment would be as a new day
My heart would be kindled every sunrise
How do you appear to be today?
Do you live in hope as I do?
Or do I simply dream
Dream of a moment, ever on the horizon.

Élyas Rivermark

As You Walk

Under a canopy of fire
Through a field of white
I would walk with you
But even now, I know not where you are.
I hope to find you in bliss
Admiration of the world in your eyes.
I pray that darkness does not cloud your mind
As you walk
Walk with Him.

I pray that the Son carries you
The Spirit surrounds your heart
And the Father knows you.

If this is how you walk
Know that I am walking with you also.
Yes, we walk not together
But as we leave the forest of darkness
Our paths might become one
Extending into the sun.
Out of darkness He brings us
With your hand I would walk
I would walk until death
Though it is only a temporary thing.
For with the Father I will love you
Into His light I will propose my love
In His presence I will make it eternal
With the Spirit I will make it whole.

My love for my Father
It is greater than my love for you.
Yet the more I love Him.
Greater is my love for you
Please believe me.
For *as you walk*
Know that he is beside you
As you walk
Know this in your heart
I would walk with you
Can you see me?

Élyas Rivermark

These Rose-Coloured Eyes

Aye
I believe still in the power of love
True love's existence does not hide from me.
In my eyes it remains for all eternity
Adding a tint of roses
To a world that strives to be so blue.
True love guides my heart
It is what gets me through the day
And especially the night.
To a woman I would give myself
Though it would take great effort.
I may only think of roses
But my eyes are not blinded.
Reality can be beautiful
Real love, when true, burns so bright.
I would continue to fight
Fight for her beyond death.

These eyes of mine have betrayed
They lied to me in times of love.
But I do not regret those times
My eyes saw love, perhaps not true.
They were an experience of the heart
The growth of my desire to love
Anything more and it would have been true.
To those that I have given my heart to:
You received real love
All of me, you had it
Yet not strong enough to be true.
Why must I give everything?
Yet to me they only give half?

I know that you will give me everything.
For you I will give myself.

Nay
I do not believe in a mate of my soul,
For there are too many to count.
There are many that complete me…
Many that form who I have become:
A friend that does not leave,
A man of the best kind,
There are those who are always
Always with me at every step.

Aye
You are a different kind
True love means so much more.
Someone I would spend every moment
Trying to be the best for you.
For the best is what you deserve
Through *these rose-coloured eyes*
I see you as God intended
Beautiful beyond compare..
Within and without, I am speechless.
Let my eyes do the talking.
Some may say that they have been clouded
That I cannot see the truth.
These rose-coloured eyes
They are not evil
It does not hurt me to see the good
For you are good for me
Always will be.

Élyas Rivermark

Hair Like Flames

She is the ultimate contrast
With *hair like flames* in the night
A smile brighter than the sun.
Her eyes are like the sea
So calm, pearls of blue that delve deep.
A dress of the brightest red
I know her not enough
Only that she is the Lord's.
Like her hair, her heart burns so bright
For Him
But that is enough…

They Will Never Understand

Often, love is given a simple name.
It is but a feeling, nothing more.
Something that forms simply out of proximity.
I love her, simply because I do
I love her, simply because I must.
An explanation of love is complex
They will never understand.

Love cannot be explained by the word itself
Nor does the feeling suffice.
It comes from something else.
An experience, but also a connection
Without a sense of things shared
Time spent together, yes
But also a connection of similarity.
The idea of opposite attraction
It has merit.
Though an opposite in one aspect
Will ruin even the greatest attraction.
To think…
There is a base level at which love may exist.
This base level may be superseded
Many enemies become friends, allowing love to flourish.
I digress…
To understand romantic love is near impossible.

Élyas Rivermark

Indeed, love has no bounds
I have searched for the ends of its strings
No end exists in this world.
No task is impossible through love, one that is true.
What is true?
Verily, I do not know, I have not felt it.

But that of the soul?
I have felt those that have changed me
For them, I had done so much
Many hearts would have run out
My love is never ending
It does not go dry.
It only changes
With each new heart it becomes anew.
Do you understand?

Many men speak of being broken.
I believe them.
But *they will never understand*
Being broken is not a trait
It is but a choice.
We can choose to love, or to hate.
A hate that often fuels revenge.
But what of love?
So much more power in it.
If you love them
You will see how you changed them
And how they changed you.
Therefore,
Do not hate those that broke you.
For *they will never understand.*

By Your Light I Must Live

I live in the light
In the light of my God
Blissful until the ends of the Earth.
In his light I will endure.
I will delight in it.

In your light
In your light is something different
A piece of me lives in you
More than I want it to.
Yet it fills me with such a current.
Into you I pour my God-given love
Every aspect of you fills my heart
I cannot see you
For years you have been far from me
But, your light reaches me.
The love in your heart explodes.
The beauty of your smile
The glint in your eyes
They pierce my already dying heart.
My soul yearns for you.
By your light I must live.

Élyas Rivermark

Here I Drown

Under a sea of tears I dwell
Shed by mine own eyes
Shed for those I professed to love.
Truth be told
I am not a saint, imperfect by nature
I have lied, I have hurt
Never once did I cheat.
Yet I find my soul weeping.
Time has not been kind to my heart
Every crack growing deeper
Why can I not let go?

Here I drown
My lips, stained red by the fruit of the vine.
Remembering all of the hearts
Hearts which I had discovered
By their fire I was kept warm.
A heart of stone, finally warm to hold.
One by one
Piece by piece
They took shards for themselves.

It was not theft, I gave them freely
Now I have so few left
Each piece of me in their hand
Though they know it not
They will hold it for a full life
Unaware that I go with them.
A piece of my heart lives within their own
So *here I drown*
The lives of those I have loved bearing down.

A Lament of the Heart

The heat of jealousy, always hot within me.
Why did they not try?
Am I so easily cast aside?

No

No

It was not fated to be so.
What mark have I left on them?
Am I a source of pain?
A source of sorrow indeed.

So quickly come and gone
I left no mark at all.
I see them smiling
A pang of sorrow thrusts into my heart.
My mind knows better
I know to be joyful in gladness.
For they have true happiness
Something that I could not provide.
There are many who need me not
That itself is painful to bear.
In all my years of life
I have not met the one with the will
Nor the understanding to love me.

Do not be mistaken
I do not believe I am hard to love
Not like many tend to believe.
I rather like to drown myself.
In work
In life
It is difficult for me to not become bored.

Élyas Rivermark

The monotony of some loves
They allow me to find a way to escape.
I become bored
The same conversation day by day
Running through my head.
I know what they are going to say
Why bother?

Here I drown
Forever in the monotony of talking
Never going further than the casual.
Mind you, I have tried to break the cycle
To endeavour toward romantic gestures.
They are always destroyed
Wasted on a petty heart.
Wasted by an uninvested soul.

Why do I continue to try?
It has become clear to me
I am not doomed to be alone
Nor doomed to die.
Yet *here I drown*
Knowing that I am doomed
Doomed to wait
Wait and listen for them to come
For then…
Then I will drown
Drown her in love.
Finally…

A smile upon my face.

The Rain Upon My Face

Here I am in my home
Remembering
Remembering things lost to time.
Moments within my dying heart that fade
Into shades of black and white.
I cannot bring colour into their memory.
For to my heart, they have lost their light
Receding into but a dull memory.

I am not alone in my plight
But alone have I succumbed
Succumbed to the ever-crushing weight
One that was brought on by my love.
So much
I cannot bear to rest my eyes on you.
Aye
Lost to time and bland
But the wounds continue to fester.
For when I see your smile
It does not set my heart alight.
It had once burned for you.

In a wave of tears
You destroyed my heart.
A few have tried to put it back together
All failed to repair its destruction.

I have become timid in my despair
Giving only pieces of the pieces away
None have handled them with care
Only pain.

Élyas Rivermark

Do you see what you have done?
Reduced my memories to ashes.
Cold
The flame that had once burned
Only a painful memory.

Do you remember?
I had promised myself to you.
It was to be us
Absorbed by the gravity of love.
I had not known
A universe could be something on Earth.

Do you remember?
As we walked
We shared every step.
You asked me to stop.
A universe of our own making
There on that bridge
Each person but a passing mist.
In your eyes I saw the stars
A smile upon your lips.
We kissed like the rain.

You said you were leaving
I asked how could that be
Not another sentence left your lips
At least, not one I wish to remember.
Only three words
Three I wish were never spoken.

A Lament of the Heart

There I am on that bridge
Remembering
Remembering your kiss
The way your hand rested on my cheek
The slight tinge of red around us
Covering us in a rose-coloured glow.
It was gloomy and grey that day
But as we walked
Our universe shone so bright.

Do you remember?
That red umbrella
That beautiful red dress
In my memories of ash
It remains the only tint of colour
As you will always be to me
A rose among the thorns.

Here I am in a field of green
It is so bright and so colourful
So why?
Why must I only see grey?
Your smile was like the sun
I only wish to see it once more
These flowers that I hold
Images of your umbrella
They bring the only colour to my life.

Please won't you come back to me
I cannot live this life alone
Though spring is on its way
I lay these roses at your gravestone.
The sun shines on a field of stone
Where so many flowers bloom

So why?

Why do I feel *the rain upon my face?*
Remembering,
Remembering those three words.

I am dying…

With These Secrets

Dearest Beloved,

I want to tell you a secret, perhaps a few in this short time I have with you. I am younger than I seem. My experience of this life is not as robust as my words show. The meanings of my poems can be derived from exact moments in my short life, they may even be traced to inspirations as simple as a painting. The feelings behind my words, however, are no less real than the pages beneath your fingers. I must confess that I have never walked that windy evening, nor have I stood in the fields of stone where the flowers bloom. Be this a fine confession: I love you more than those poems, in my heart you are the reason for these words.

I hope to find you among the thorns. The words forever enshrined on these pages will serve as a testament to the path I have taken to be by your side. It reminds me of the complexity of my own life. It is true that I see you every day. My life, it seems, is a never-ending trail of switchbacks. I look up and there you are, smiling down at me. Every hundred steps, I feel as if I must turn and follow the path that lies at my feet. I trust that this will one day end, for one day, I will no longer need to write.

In those days, my words will take on a very different tone. All these years praying, breaking, and weeping, they will not be wasted. To be with you, to be your husband, my heart will forever be light.

The Knight of Your Heart,

Élyas

Élyas Rivermark

Here in This Bed With You

I am scared…

I have been so, for many a year.
Of what?
Well

Of Love…

In my heart I know you
But mine heart does betray me
For I am a broken man
Aye
The cracks are unseen by all
Love boiling under the surface.
It is wild now, piercing all things
No control
No interest
My spark has gone out
An inferno in its place.

Shall I tell you a story?
I had loved so intensely once
Blind and reckless
But it was true.

In the end it tore away from me
Leaving a heart of stone.
Aye
It can blaze as it once did
As a phantom, a mere image
That true love of old is gone.

A Lament of the Heart

My darling,
As I lie here
Here in this bed with you
I want to chase that love
I want to give it to you freely
Though it continues to evade my grasp.
Slipping more each moment
Until it is gone.
No control
No interest
That love is truly gone from me
So, what can take its place?

In this new life I ask for one
One moment of true love.
Not like before
Something new and green within me.
I know not what it is
But I do know one thing
I am empty.
So please
Be patient with me.

Here in this bed with you
I do not know how to love
Not anymore
I am too broken.
I am healing
Please be patient
Here in this bed with me.

Élyas Rivermark

Jealousy and Envy

There are maladies in this world
Ones that do no physical harm
They do so much more damage.
Jealousy
It has consumed them
Can they not see the rot?

What is a jealous heart's purpose
Other than death?
The scarlet rot that consumes the light
Leaving only a void of anger and *envy*
I do not fear death
Only a jealous heart.
Bringing sorrow in its wake
You would bring tears?
Solely to fulfil your own insecurities?
Have you no sense of pride?
Of all the souls in this world
They chose yours.
Take them into your arms
Show them your strength.

Aye,
There will be doubt
Even I am not immune to its grasp
Envy is a dangerous poison
Instead of the seeds of love
It sows those of anger and pain.
Let it not touch your heart
Lest it begin to fester.

Please, hold them close
Be not afraid of those that care
For it can be a beautiful blessing
A blessing to have other guardians of their heart.
Instead use your pride as a shield
Do not let it become a sword to stab another
They may lose faith in you
Do not isolate them from others.
A broken heart cannot love
Show them your strength
Prove you are a match to their heart.
I am confident you can do so.

A jealous heart does not live.
It festers and rots from within
Leaving a husk
Anger and hatred oozing beneath the surface.
How could they love such a thing?
Instead, shine like a beacon
Show them your beauty
Others cannot take them
If they only have eyes for you.
Show them your faith
And they cannot be unfaithful
If they are…

Was it really love?

Élyas Rivermark

This Beaten Path

How long has it been?
Roaming this cave of sorrow.
I see the lights now and again
Off my own *beaten path.*
They are not for me to follow
Let some other soul find their comfort.

How long have I walked this path?
Not knowing what each step holds
I do not care.
Oh how I have stumbled
Many times struggling to rise again.
Yet, there have been so many hands
Lifting me up, bearing a light.
Some are lost souls, same as I
Others, false guides.
I always return to this path
For it is not laid out by my own hand.
Though beaten
It is Divine.

At times I see the light at the end
Oh how beautiful it is.
It shines not as the sun
But gentle as a distant star
A sweet caress after a long road.

I long for that sweet caress
A release from my pain and my guilt
From my shame and my sorrow
It waits for me, along *this beaten path.*

A Lament of the Heart

Lord, let there be a light
Be with me throughout this life.
I know I will stumble and stray
But by your light I may find it
That sweet caress of death
I do not fear it
For there is sweet life after death.

In this life
May you walk with me
But please, let there be another.
One who is not perfect
One who stumbles and strays.
They walk a path next to my own
I cannot see it
So would you join us together?
By Your light I am able to move
With another hand I may run.
Alive once again.

Too long have I walked
In bitterness and in anger
From one who claimed to love me
So I ask…let me love again
Destroy this wall around me
Soften my heart.
May I give them my hand?
May we walk together?
In this darkness
Stumbling and straying
Only to come back to you, loving you.
Together until we reach that sweet caress
At the end of *this beaten path.*

Élyas Rivermark

Waiting On You

The slow passage of time
We often do not feel it around us.
Slowly wearing away all things
But there is a moment
A time when it is agonising.
In waiting we feel its passage
The slow crawl of every second
Every moment feels like an eternity.

There is another more agonising thing.
It is waiting, *waiting on you*
No, not while I have you
For that would be bliss.
It is the moments when I do not
It is those when I do not know you
Or those when I do
Waiting on you to see the love in me.

It is waiting to see you.
Giving my love to those that do not want it.
Giving all of my heart
Only to have it toyed with.
Please save me from these wicked women
Those that only wish to play games.
Let my love fall on your ears
Hear my words of adoration.
Hold me in your heart
For I shall die there.

But I am *waiting on you,* slowly
Step by step, day by day.

With Hope

To be a hopeless romantic
Often it is given the wrong semantic
For it is not to be full of hopelessness
But rather to have hope in excess
To believe in bygone things
True love, romance, and chivalry
Modern love, what is this devilry?
We are not made for it.
So…
With Hope
I wait for you
With Hope
We have many things to do.

Élyas Rivermark

On the Nature of Our Hearts

Dearest Beloved,

I have discovered something on the nature of the human heart. I have found that we are not built for this modern world. An epidemic of indifference and promiscuity has ravaged the world. Now, before you say anything, please listen to my words.

God created love, in fact, Love is God's greatest creation. I believe in the sanctity of it and I find the claim of my own prudishness to be ill-founded. I believe that the strong sense of sexual love is important to our own humanity. The Song of Solomon often comes to mind in these moments. Both the man and the woman describe each other's features in mesmerising detail. In searching for you, I dream of a time when we may do that for each other. Unfortunately, this world we live in is poisonous. From a young age, I had access to every aspect of a woman, pictures and videos so easily at my fingertips. I became indifferent to the divine beauty of the women around me, instead using my heartbreak as an excuse to use them for myself. It is sad that this behaviour is applauded. This modern world cares only for the pervasiveness of a man's sexual exploits. The supposed strength of men and women comes from the amount of beds they have experienced. Chastity is looked down upon, indeed, I wish I could go back and escape this hole I have created for myself.

Our hearts are not built to withstand this type of modern "love". I have found that a small piece of myself is left within every woman's bed I have lain. I find my mind drifting to images of them, my own actions haunt my dreams. I pray everyday that I might forget their touch, forget the night I spent, itching to drive home. It may only be me who feels this way, but my heart feels bored and brittle now. I wish I could apologise to the hearts I used for my own satisfaction, the boredom I felt with the bodies that lay beneath me. I have changed, I cannot bear to do that to someone ever again, instead, I want to be enamoured with love once more, I want to gaze upon you with new eyes each day.

I pray for those like me, for those that fell into the trap that this world has set. I know there are others who have dirtied themselves with indifference in an effort to achieve temporary ecstasy. I also ask for forgiveness, forgive me for my past, a past full of wandering eyes and insatiable lust. I have forsaken that life, instead asking for one of old, a time when we as men and women gave ourselves to only one other. To many I sound like a hopeless romantic, in truth I am so full of hope, I believe this world is like a pendulum. It tends to swing the other way after some time to itself. We may soon understand that believing in this modern love has broken many young people. I see it day by day: a sense of hopelessness, a lack of communication, and an unhealthy fixation on validation. I know I may sound old fashioned, but I am a family man, my criteria to find someone is so simple:

Love God
Love Your Family
Love Me

And please, please make the effort to love, everything else will fall into place shortly after.

The Knight of Your Heart

Élyas

Élyas Rivermark

Weathering This Rain With You

For better and for worse
Feelings that puncture my joyful heart
It is so easy to experience the betters
Where are we in the worst?
Modern love is so fickle
Fleeing at the very thought of hardship.
Darling, I am not so shallow.
Berate me with words.
Raise your voice.
Let your anger roll over me.
Forever shall I remain.

In love I came to you
Come, let me wipe these tears away
Let your anger turn to comfort.
Forever I will hold you
Evermore in a loving embrace
'Til death do us part.
I would walk with you now
Into this storm of life
Hold onto me as I hold onto you.

The tears of heaven may fall
I do not fear them.
When evil comes for our fragile hearts
Look to me, we shall both look upward.
These tears do not bode ill
For like a phoenix, it is a remedy.
They speak of a calm before
But let us bring it in time.

In sickness
I put my trust in you
You make me well
By the power of your embrace.
My darling
As the Lord said
There is a time for everything
Everything under the sun.
Please do not fear this rain
For it is but a passing thing.
Look for beauty within the clouds
Peace in the kiss of their tears.

I would kiss you like the rain
If I knew it would bring joy.
I would embrace you
If I knew it would bring you healing.
Please let me into your heart
Do not be frightened
I only wish to breath life
Reignite your beautiful spark.
For it may rid us of this awful storm
To see you blaze as before.

Until that moment
I am not afraid
Every moment, you bring me life.
For better and for worse
Sickness and health
I am with you
Loving you with all that I have

Weathering this rain with you

Could I Hold You

I do not want anything more
But to hold you in my arms.
O Lord
Into my arms, would you lead her?
When she's tired of running
I want to take away the hurt.
Please forgive me
I do not have the words
So let me hold you.

One day I may kiss you
I know this to be true
I am so scared of that day.
For it to be special
To be decidedly us
When I do, I know it was to be you.
I cannot do it now.
So please
Could I hold you?

One day we may be one
Under the light of the moon.
That night must be sanctified
It cannot happen before
For I know now how it must be.
Every urge must be fought
For indeed, it will be a fight.
But Lord, I want to do this right
So please, as we wait for that blessed night
Let me hold you.

Even when I am hurting
On my deathbed I might be
I would hold you until my dying breath.
For every breath I breathe
I pray you would hear it.
Let my arms give you comfort
For it is all that I can do.
Oh angel on Earth
I cannot do anything more
Than wrap my arms around you
Hold you tight
Every emotion seeped out of me.
Joy, peace, and love, let them flow into you.
Take away the hurt.
Please give it to me
Let it melt away.

Every moment with you I fight a smile
Too long has it been
Since I have fallen in love so foolishly.
A message from you
Brings forth such a profound grin
Why must it be this way?
I can do nothing to keep it at bay
So please
Could I hold you tonight?
If you allow me but a moment
I may just melt into you
So please, let me hold you.

Élyas Rivermark

A Hug (Once More)

Many times I will try to explain it.

A hug will suffice when something is missing
Comfort when someone is reminiscing
In times of romance you may prefer a kiss
But as before, it will be something to dismiss.
To feel their arms wrap around your chest
Somehow it feels better than the honey of the lips.
A gentle heartbeat in tune with my own
I believe it would be just fine.

How quickly a kiss becomes passion and lust
A hug may keep a layer of trust.
There are times when a kiss is right
Within an embrace upon the brow
For reasons beyond me, it somehow means more.
I do not condemn a kiss
Please do not misunderstand
As with everything, it has a time and place.
But *a hug?*
That can be shared with anyone.

Oh how I love so completely
A hug I would give to every soul
With time I could make it my goal.

Into her arms I would run
To fall into an embrace for so long
I wish she would hold me in life
Then I may conquer any amount of strife.

Into the arms of my friends
It is there where I find my worth.
They love me in every moment
I only wish they would hold me forever.

In the arms of my father I would die
For at the end I would feel safe
Safe to join others in heaven
On Earth as it is above
My father's arms are a haven from the world.

True love was created from my mother
A hug from her heals even the deepest wounds
A broken heart
As I lie here bleeding
My angel of a mother is my saving grace
I am free to live in her embrace.

From my brothers and sisters *a hug* is different
Its beauty is so awkward
But its strength is unmatched.
We may bicker and fight
But I would give my life so they may yet live.
It is the greatest gift to give
As I embrace a brother or a sister
I know that we are the same.

A hug is so much more than an embrace
I may wrap my arms around you
But it is my heart that touches you
With every beat I hope for an embrace
Because it just might be another's saving grace.

Élyas Rivermark

Do not underestimate the power of a touch
It could be the one thing that brings them back
One touch that takes them away from the edge.
Forever I will hug often
Everyday I will seek it out
For it is one of the beauties of this world
To be caught in an embrace
One moment that feels safe
To feel loved
My soul yearns for it.

A hug is a blessing.
Without words they will understand
Spend forever within *a hug*
The heart will know what the other needs.

By Your Grace

As the leaves change to red and gold
The crisp wind tugging
I walk to feel the sand on my feet
The soft scratch of wool on my back
Looking at You.
I write to You now by the fire
All things You have created
Every wonderful detail
By your grace
Given to me.
With every passing breath
Falling ever more in awe of You.

Élyas Rivermark

I Choose You

You are not the most beautiful in the world
Indeed you are not the most perfect
You have blemishes and scars.
Where there is pain there are cracks
Stone walls surround your heart
But in my world
In the garden of my mind
My love, you are the most gorgeous flower.
Forever I will look at you
Admiration and love in my eyes
For me?
You are the most beautiful
The most perfect
In all your flaws
I will always love you.

In the pain of this life
The sadness and the joy
I will be with you always
To the ends of the earth
May death take me.
I choose you.

Patiently Fading

In fact, I know I am not here long
A day may come when I am whole
Solid in a place where I belong
Safe with my heart that you stole.
Yet here I am
Giving piece after piece
Hoping to find you among the thorns
Until then
I am *patiently fading.*
A shadow in the hearts of many
Many whom I had given my heart to.

Élyas Rivermark

This Crystal Forest

To cross that threshold is to enter another.
A place dancing with the lights of heaven.
On clouds of satin and silk they lie
Waiting for just the right heart
To take them away from this place.
To shine into the life of another.

As you walk *this crystal forest*
Discover the colours.
Red rubies clutched so tightly in gold.
Some, the colour of the blood of roses
Others bear the glint of fire.
None compare to the one
The one only I can see.
It shines like the red star
So mellow and content.
It does not call to me
It is for another hand to caress
Special to another, as it should be.
I may pass it by, but beautiful it remains
Waiting patiently for another to bless.

I see fields of deep green
Stretching out before me, glittering in the light of day.
They shone on silver branches
Beckoning my heart.
With the softness of moss
A deep colour of seaweed in my eyes
I was born in these fields
Could I not return to them?
As I stood, I could not fathom my return

A Lament of the Heart

Those deep shades of green…
Though they are mine
They will not fulfil this need.

Pulling away from the sea of green
My eyes rested upon their own.
A forest of blue so rich, I could feel a tear drift away.
Such joy from something so blue
If it was another day
I may have approached this forest.
But like the sea of green
I could not enter the sky of blue
I did not have the wings to fly.
My quest pulled me further.

Quickly did I make my way through the never ending stars
So clear and crisp
I could not stand it.
They were as unique as water
Some muddy, or tainted pink.
They would never do.

Past the waves of purple.
The treasure of the sea.
Iridescent clouds drifting between
No.
Only one would do in this forest.
One crystal that I could grasp.

At last at the end of my path
I saw what lay beneath me.
A crowd of amber and gold
Smouldering in their cocoons.
I was alone with these, rapture overtaking my heart

Élyas Rivermark

At last I had found my embrace
To my own emerald heart.

I could feel its call
A crystal not the same
But a compliment to my eyes
To my heart it beckoned.

This is the one that I must choose.
I was wandering in *this crystal forest*
Searching for only one, one to grace your hand.
May it be an extension of your heart.
In a forest of so many stars
Only your light shines brightest.
From this forest I stole you,
There are days that I feel selfish.
I choose you.

It makes me wonder
Did you search this forest for green?
Perhaps not…
It is not a forest for you to search
So I must ask
Would you accept this heart of green?
The eyes of blue to adore you?
Forevermore
Else I must wait once more
Endless days in *this crystal forest.*

As a Sprite You Lead Me

Chasing you is like trying to catch the wind.
Running in every direction
Like a leaf in the breeze
A smile forever on your face.

Here under this moon
I hope to see your heart
Eyes like starlight
A smile so dangerous.
Are you a Siren in my ears?
Here to lure me into my own fall.
Unlike Odysseus
I do not have protection from you.
If you steal away my heart
Keep it for yourself.
I do not fear the fall
A warm embrace
Shattering the cold depths I have fallen into.

As I walk through this forest of life
Like a nymph you call out to me
A hero of old am I not?
Chasing after the sound of your voice
Hoping to one day catch you.
I will hold you close, hold you in my arms.
This life is so beautiful, I only wish to share it.
So let me fall against your skin
With you I may fight the demons
Only for you, a hero in your life and mine.

But in truth,
As a sprite you lead me
Only ever close enough to see
Yet always out of reach
Oh, how you tease me.
I cannot help falling in love with you
Every breath stolen from my chest
You pull them from me.
I would freely give it
So please, would you hold me
Under these old oak trees?

Just as the breeze touches my face
So does your kiss
Kiss me so I know it is true
That you will no longer let me chase you
But to finally catch the wind.
"Leave her wild"
I do not bear your chains
Only to ask for your hand
By my life I will hold it.

For *as a sprite you lead me*
Past these Sirens,
Your hands like muffs, blocking their call.
You shield my eyes
Looking at your face is enough,
The nymphs have no power over me.
I want more of you.
I cherish the wind, as it carries me through life
I do not wish for another
For I have fallen completely for you.

Dreams of a Dance

As I lie here
The purr of strings play in my ear
Yet there is no music.
Dreams of a Dance
How I wish to be in that embrace
Only your face in a sea of fog
How we danced to the keys
A smile forever on our face.
Now it is dark
Dreams, fading into a memory
I wish they had never left me.

Élyas Rivermark

These Walls I Build

They stand so high in my heart
Reaching for the heavens
They do more than their part
So why must they fall?
So small a hand brings them down
From the depths of my heart they explode.
Perhaps I could wear the pieces as a crown.
The world should know their weakness
As strong as a promise may be
These fallen walls will destroy me.

My heart felt as if it could love again
So fierce yet so different
It did not cling as it once did.
No longer on gaudy and shallow display
For its cracks were not so deep
They could be filled by the right hand.
She filled them
And more.
The man I ought to be
No longer lusting as before.
True love it could have been for me
In the storm looking toward the shore.

Every moment spent building walls
The light of my heart dimmed
But one cannot control who falls.
I love you
More than I should
You tore down my walls
Every last one smashed to bits.

I would break yours if I could
But they are a maze, by my strength I cannot find a way.
Confused am I, loving every day
Greatness comes to those who wait.
I wait on the Lord.
His patience exceeds my own
So please
Give me patience
Let me love her…
So I may let her love me.
In time I wait
For better or worse
This time, it is by my own hand that I break
These walls I build

Élyas Rivermark

Why Does it Hurt

The world is tearing me apart
How they hurt, these matters of the heart.
My heart finally softened
I began to give it away once more.
Each piece bringing more love
So much joy burned within me
With such gentle hands she took them
Her smile smouldering in my memory
She was never mine
I knew that.
So, how could I fall?

Why does it hurt?
I knew in my heart she was not mine
Nor would she ever be
Her smile pulled me in
Her touch calmed my anxious soul
I let myself love her.
My heart acted on its own.
No…
I chose to love her
I still choose to love her
Though it hurts me so
Please make it stop!
I want to forget….

Broken Promises

The pieces of my heart break so often
I do not notice the cracks
Webs spreading further every minute
Deepening and rotting still.
Do you know this feeling?
So many promises made
Every one, broken in time
A piece of me, torn away
Memories like ash on my tongue.
Tasteless and grey,
Her words were never enough.

She should not say that she loved me
Lies have no substance.
Instead of gold, she repaired my heart with poison
Why do I drink it in?
These promises make me fall
Blind to the evil in my eye.
Am I at fault?
Putting these words into her mouth
Forcing her to promise to me
Something she could not give.
Perhaps it is not her who did the breaking.

They are my own creation
My voice coming back to me through her
These *Broken Promises*
They come from a broken heart
Like shells
They are brittle and thin
No substance, no weight.

Élyas Rivermark

May I make a new promise?
I promise to wait for you
I will not put words into your mouth
I will not be broken
Repair my heart from its pieces
Bring colour back into my life.

One day I will ask…
Will you make me a promise?
Will you hold my heart?
Different than any other?

It will no longer be broken
The cracks will have become scars
It will be full, scarred, but strong.
Will you hold it?
Keep it for yourself
Please
Make me a promise
The last one I wish to hear.
Will you promise to love me?
Every blemish and scar so ugly
One day healed by angels.

A heart that beats for you
I am not the man I once was
I trust him more than me
So please
In a world of *broken promises*
Know this to be true
My promise finally has life
The day you hold my heart
I will never speak for you.

Broken Promises no longer have power
I have been freed
To see you through my eyes
A heart alight, like new
I promise you
Truly, I love you.

Élyas Rivermark

Come Back to Me

Come back to me
I cannot bear this broken winter wasteland
Please reignite that gentle fire in your heart
The one that coaxes me to finally stand
I will always love you as is my part.
As I stare at your picture I see a sea
Not of water as you might expect
Expect instead one of flames
Flames of love that burn bright.
Bright as can be.

You're in pain, that much is clear
Love hurts, and with distance is full of despair
Yet while I still breathe, I give you everything.
When I look at you, I can only stare.
Tears run down my face, urged by the joy you bring.
For years, I prayed, God's answer quells the fear
He sent me you
You who came in a torrent of love
Love that surpasses all doubt
Doubt that no longer lives here.

I will wait forever for your soul,
You have taken mine, with love and with delight
I gave it to you to hold until the end
A piece within me still, burning with your light
Please, do not take it away,
Without it I may begin to bend
Depression rising, beginning to take its toll
Without you I may break.
Break and become as I once existed

Existed with God, yet a piece seemed lost.
Lost not from me, but from the world.

Come back to me, my angel of love
I promised God I would never leave
I am open to you and will always be here.
My feelings written clearly on my sleeve
Family and friends may laugh or sneer
But I do not care
I promise to wait forever
Forever as long as I live
Live until you come
Come back to me.

Not Just Married

For decades I have waited
Oh how it hurt me so.
A little boy
So desperate to be a man
Standing in front of Heaven and Earth
Promising his heart and soul to another
Is there not so much more?

Two lives truly become one
Every moment spent together
Together or apart
It does not matter.
I would have another to share my soul.
No secret can be safe
That is how it is meant to be.

It is not meant to be easy
Do not misunderstand
I know the hours of work.
Days working to make it right
Two souls becoming one.
Aye…That is one messy affair.
It requires not just one death
But two people dying to themselves.
An ultimate sacrifice
One made with an eternal mate
One sworn to be with you forever.
When I weep, she is there
When I have so much joy
Best of all
I may spend all those moments with you.

I want *not just married*
I want every fight
To see you at the end of your rope
To cry with you
Laugh, and be angry.
Love is not just the big moments,
It is choosing you at every moment.
I will never stop choosing you,
Over and over.

I do not want to marry just anyone.
No
I choose you.
You have my heart and my breath.
I want to see you be a mother
I want to see your mess
Every colour and shape of you.
Not just married
Truly one body
Fighting everyday to be better
Seeing even deeper
Living for the moment.

If I could relive my life
Every new life
I would find you.
I would keep coming back
Through anger, hurt or sorrow
I would follow you.

So.
Would you marry me?

Élyas Rivermark

Vows to Your Heart

Dearest Beloved,

You have heard my pleas and you have read the words carved on my heart. Would you please accept these vows as a testament of my love for you?

I will love God more than I will love you, for if I may love Him with every fibre of my being, that love will be reflected by His grace onto you. I will be as the moon, shining so bright into your darkness. It is not a light of my own and it never will be.

Do not dismay, my love for you will not cease, for in this moment I am making a promise to you. It is not a contract to be burned in the wake of hardship. I am here forever, I will love you with every last breath, even onto my deathbed, my last breath will be spent speaking your beautiful name.

I do not believe in cowardice, therefore, I will not cheat. Like divorce, these words will never leave my mouth, now will I never speak of such things in jest. I am for you, and you are for me.

I will always speak to you, in anger and in weeping, in joy and in ecstasy, I will spend every moment with you. These emotions are important but they shall never hurt you. For if they do, I am not a man worthy of your respect.

In every way, I will provide for you, from this very minute I will hold myself responsible for your well-being. I pray that you are joyous in this life, but I understand that there are times when you will need comfort. My arms are forever open to you.

As Christ loved the church, I am not afraid to die in your place. I will always come between you and any form of danger so that you might live. Be that as it may, I will always live for you, each day admiring what we have built.

For years I have prayed for this day, the day when we may start our own eternity. I do not fear it.

More vows will come when I know I have met you, there will be things in this life that only you need. Happily I will always give them. Already you have transformed my heart. No longer do I waste my time with those that seek to break my heart and steal my body. The cracks and wounds that once riddled my body are only silvery wisps upon my skin. Whole I will come to you, strong and courageous in your eyes.

Until that day,

I patiently await your beautiful smile.

The Knight of Your Heart

Élyas

Élyas Rivermark

God's Beauty

This world is dark.
There are forces that move against us
Too many days are spent in suffering
I can feel it growing around me.
The world turns toward madness
It finds comfort in anger
As the Earth burns
Her people turn from joy
Letting hatred flourish in its absence.

There is fear, yes, but beauty also.
Open thine eyes and you might see
Not thine own path
But the path of God stretched before you
His beauty is unlike any other.
For His path be not easy
Only real.
Perfect for thy feet to follow.

The joy God provides is unlike any other
It is not of the body
Nor of this world
It is a joy of the soul.
That joy comes in the small moments
The little bits of God in every day.

Look at thy life.
He is always there.
There are angels behind every action
For they fight on our behalf
Though they may be delayed

The angels will always triumph.

All of this life follows its path
Winding through thorns
Rushing over rivers
Into the beauty of the heavens.
Through flames or flowers
Fear not
It is as God wills it to be.

Please, enjoy the journey.
See *God's beauty* in every detail:
A mother carrying a smiling child
A boy and a girl sharing a kiss
A family laughing in the park
Two old men remembering days past
A group of girls smiling and laughing together
A boy running late for a first date
A couple dancing, alone in a busy world
A wife smiling at a text.

Please, take in the world around you
For it is alive
Not so dark as it seems.
Too many days are spent in sorrow
Instead, look up.
Do not wallow in darkness
For you are not alone.
Take heart in experiencing life
It is more beautiful than you think.

Élyas Rivermark

A Psalm of my Own

I lift up my eyes to the night sky
By Your hand the cool rain falls
Washing away my tears and pain.
My God, you are my strength
Even now in the darkness
I feel your hand guiding me.
When I stumble, I do not fear.
The end of my path may draw near
With joy I will continue.
For when my path ends
My God you will show me your own.

Blessed are those that delight in You
As a child I come
Proof of your radiance ever on my face.
A voice to sing
Nor a body to run
Hast thou given me
But a hand to write
In words I shall shout my praises
Through my fingers let your radiance show.

Even if I may never speak
My hand shall ever glorify you.
I cannot write as David
My God, pour your love into my hand
So that I may come close
Close enough to write your truth.
So even if I must die
Your glory continues in my words on a page.

My God, when you speak
Heaven's host of angels sing
When you smile
The whole world brightens.
Blessed are those that walk in your grace
For the wrath of God is terrible.
Let us be saved from sorrow
We praise your greatness
Let us not feel your anger
For through fire we already walk
Every moment blackened by sin.
On Earth we are not holy
But through your Son
We are washed clean.

Blessed am I when I write
For your name is ever on my mind.
My God, your love hath no bounds
May it give me my faith.
Faith like Daniel, in a den of lions
May it give me hope, hope like Moses
In a long wilderness
Let your love abound in me
I would share it with the world.

As I stand here
Rain gently kissing my face
I rejoice in the life that I was given.
I trust in your holy name
May your unfailing love surround me
For there is light
Even on the gloomiest of days
Be with me now and forevermore.

Élyas Rivermark

The Little Things

Life by nature is not dark
Though there may be clouds
Have you seen their crowns?
Under a setting sun
They blaze like fires of orange and gold.
Even in the midst of darkness
The moon shines bright in the night
There is beauty in the dark
And horror in the light
Who are we to determine what is good?
All we have to decide
Is how our eyes look upon the world.

We may choose to look at Death
For he is the master of deception.
We may choose to look at Sorrow
For we so naturally follow its footsteps.
Why do we not choose Life?
For it allows us to think such things.
Why do we not choose Joy?
When we long for it everyday.
Everyday we are tempted by Death
Our focus brings our own destruction.
Let us instead choose Joy
Aye…
It may be chosen in this life
But it starts with small steps.

To see the trees in bloom
Realising that every flower is a gift
A canopy of pink and white
Growing just as it ought.
To hear the strum of a guitar
Carried on the wings of the wind
A brief serenade in a tumultuous city.
Perhaps of some lovestruck voice?
To smell that of a distant memory
Transporting through time
An image of your own past
All this takes is a moment
Stop
Allow time to return to you.

Find Joy behind moments of Anger
Of Pain and of Sorrow.
In time
Your pain may produce another's moment of joy
No
Not if they inflict pain
But if they find love, but not in you.
In victory over you
Let pride not overcome your heart.
Create your own story
Yet not to the detriment of others.

Soon you may see
That happiness is, and always will be
Behind every moment.
It begins with *the little things*
For these are small,
But can surely take your breath away.

Élyas Rivermark

Running After You

I have always seen you go before me
Beautiful in my eyes
You are my Mona Lisa
My rainbow skies
How the tears flow from me
As joy takes hold of my heart.
You will always grow
Ever more beautiful
In my eyes.

Love has always been good to me
Even in my dreams, I chase after you
If only to fall asleep with you
Awake in your arms in the morning.
It is not my time
For now I may only watch
As you dance through my memory
Your smile tells me to fall.
Oh, how I have fallen
For that beautiful smile
I have never seen one so kind
I pray to see it every day.

How the edges curve so perfectly
Seeming ever so close to a smirk.
The brightness of your eyes
They pull me in so
Though I follow you
I pray that you will turn toward me.
Turn around
Let me grow ever closer to you
Please show me that smile once more
To you, my heart is ever bound.

Running after you
Your beautiful golden hair
Bouncing with every step
Truly, I do not find it fair
To only see you from behind
For I wish only to see your face
Rest my hand on your cheek
Tell you I will never leave.

I know your heart has been broken before.
I have felt my own heart break.
Would you believe me if I told you
I will not be like him?
My love for you has no bounds
Every beat of my heart
Every heave of my chest
They are given to you.
So please
Turn around
My arms are open wide.
I will wipe away your tears
Hold you until you smile once more
You may allow all those fears to die.

Élyas Rivermark

I know you are trying
You have turned toward me before
I know you are scared
But I only bring love
I would love you forever
You need only trust me.
It will take time
I will wait for the bells to chime.
Until then I am fine
Running after you.

The Path to You

I know what He has promised to me
To be loved and to be free
I look ahead and I see you
To me the path looks so straight
For His hand is on your shoulder
Waiting for me
My path is straight
His is winding
For I must be patient in my love
Every turn and bend, I see you
One day He will give us away
To have and to hold
To love
Forever.

I Am Breaking

The time spent without you seems so short
But in my heart, *I am breaking*
I can see you, but with words I cannot speak.
I can feel you pulling away
Forsaking everything I thought we built
You feel so far away
Even when you are so close
I am breaking.

You said I was the one to tear down your walls
Yet, here I am building
You say you love me so much it hurts
But *I am breaking*
Desperately trying to build walls around my heart.
In the beginning you tore them down
With me, it has never been difficult.
Here I am now
Building walls of iron, cold as my heart.

It is strange to think that *I am breaking*
Trying to build up walls
Knowing that you are already inside
I see you in pain and that you are broken
Please let me build my walls.
You tore them down and walked inside
Let me build them around you.
These are not built out of anger nor hate
But of selfish love and foolish desire
To keep your flame within me
To warm my stone cold heart.

A Lament of the Heart

Yes, *I am breaking* that may be true
It is not dire that it was done by you
You broke me, that I can see
As I strain to rebuild
Though you are so far away
You are close to me
Letting your wild flame guide my hands
Broken, they build a fine tomb around my heart.

Élyas Rivermark

How Could I Fall Again

A heart of stone I had once
It had been softened to the core.
Such a gentle smile
I had never met one so kind.
Jaded and cold
I could never love again.
Such a warm smile
I could no longer hold that frost.
Angry and hurt,
I could never smile again.

I let myself fall
Her heart did not come to me
Another's name branded upon it
Though he did not know it
How could she not see me?
No, she saw straight into my heart
The walls could not stand against them
Such love and such affection
Piece by piece
I thought she was giving it to me.

Her heart so damaged and branded
I thought I had it.
Others told me so
In my heart I believed them.
So full of joy I had become
A smile forever fixed to my face
A heart so heavy
Soared through the heavens
No longer falling like a stone.

A Lament of the Heart

A cold and empty cave,
Now a heart, blazing so bright.

No more

Hot tears stream down my face
I had fallen
The ground swept from beneath me.
Perhaps I should have seen it
Blinded by her smile
Only listening to her laugh
I could not feel it.
I made a promise to myself,
I would not let anyone in again
Too many scars
Too many festering wounds.
How many times must I suffer from them?
How many times must I be burned?
Where stone had been
Only ash remains.

Please God, rebuild my heart
Like a phoenix, give me a new life.
I cannot bear these wounds.
So many lies
I fall for them every time.
A shadow of love is all I ever get
A shadow that quenches my fire
I am killed more each time.
For more of my heart is given
I trusted her
I thought she trusted me.

How could I fall again?

Élyas Rivermark

To You, Everything

To love is to choose
In it we may fall
At first we love the fall.
Our hearts floating like a feather
But like a tree I stood tall
Unyielding in times of bad weather.
Don't you understand?
Here I am escaping depravity
In your love I have somewhere to land
No longer do I fear love's gravity.
May I breathe again once more
For it is no feat nor a chore.

My love, you know how I fear my own breath.
A cage forever around my chest.
Every waking hour
Spent breathing, but no rest.
Even in my dreams the air comes to devour.
I do not fear death
Only the struggle to breathe
Would you take that from me?

My dear, when I am with you
Every breath comes like wind
Gusts in and out with the bellows
Feeding the fire of my heart
Brighter still does it burn for you.

To you?
Every breath in my chest
The drum of my beating heart
The tremor of my hands as they reach for your face.
Every embrace
My sorrow and my pain
Joy and healing
Every moment I give to you.
Would you please take it?

With each heave of my chest
I know that I am living
Forgive me.
For sometimes I forget
I do not want to breathe
Sometimes it is only pain
A stab beneath my ribs
How it hurts me so.
Short, painful breaths always follow
A brief moment of pain
Becoming too frequent with every day.
Would you take it from me?

Look at the man before you,
He is broken
Yet his heart is whole
His body trembles and aches
But his soul has no hole.

Élyas Rivermark

With these trembling hands
A chest that does not breathe as it ought
In this broken body
I will love you with everything.
For you, I would not tremble
For you, I could breathe.
In this world
There is nothing I would not give
To you?
Everything

You Do Not Want Me

A curse upon my chest
It is a scar
Invisible to everyone but me.

When I say "I love you"
It is not so with only part
I adore you with all that I have.
It is a curse I bear
Always to love with everything
Even when someone has nothing.
It is a broken and cracked gem
But still, I give it to them.

Love is patient, Love is kind
A line that remains in my mind
It is true.
I see only the greatest in your heart
Too many chances, some might say
But
I would give my heart a thousand times
Even though it hurts me so.

There is only one who returns a gift to me
A gift of gold for my brokenness.
My Father in heaven,
Let your love flow through me
Though my flesh may break
Harden my heart to those thorns
The ones seeking to break me.

Yet

Élyas Rivermark

I ask for one blessing
Let me love them
I want to give my heart away.
With these scars I bear
Lift the curse upon my chest
Let the wounds remain.
If I should die
Let the love I feel remain.

To the lights in my life
I know you do not love me
Not as I would die for you.
In my every breath
I think about you.
My deepest desire with every heave
Is that today, you will not leave
I wish only joy upon you
In everything that you do.

I know that *you do not want me*
In every moment I want to see you
If I should die
That will not change
On blessed wings I will fly
My hand forever on your shoulder.
If only I could also hold her.
A scar I will always bear
Love and not be loved
Give and not receive
The hearts of them do not care.

A Lament of the Heart

Forever will I love
I would give everything
Blessed is the scar I carry
My life is not my own
I know who wants me
but …
I know *You do not want me.*

But What If I Do

You told me never
Those words of yours said no.
So why did you try to steal a kiss?
It is something I try not to miss.
Was everything just for show?
You told me not to fall
To love you would only bring hurt
You told me not to break your wall
Not to love you…
But what if I do?

This Broken Body

For all my life I have been afraid
Afraid to breathe.
Whether through pain or anxiety
I could not fill my chest
I could not fill it with strength
For the strength I show is false.
Breath upon shaky breath
My lungs ached for me
More than my fragile chest could give.

There is little of my heart that remains
Shattered countless times
By those who did not mean for its destruction.
Piece by piece
I try to put it back together again
But with each shock
More pieces become lost
Taken by the hand that broke them.

Blessed are those that reach out
A hand extended to me
Offering to pull me from my pain.
I dare not reach out
I have not the strength to give
I do not want them to see my hands.
Their tremor shows my weakness
A manifestation of my broken heart
Trembling in tune with my fragile breath.

Élyas Rivermark

This broken body
Had it remained empty
Would have been reduced to ash,
My strength instead resides in my soul
It lives in the grace given to me.
Each day I walk beside Him
He who gifted me this grace.
For there are days when I cannot stand
I cannot rise
The pain in my chest is too great
Hands shaking mercilessly.
He pulls me up
Puts breath into my lungs
A holy peace in my hands.
Yes, a body still broken
But knit together with strings of light.
The brilliance of His power washes it away
All the pain
Every sorrowful moment
He takes it from me.

My darling,
I only ask this once
Will you take *this broken body?*
A chest that cannot breathe
Hands that tremble?
My heart is so strong
My soul is so bright.
Do not look at my body.
For within, it is shattered
Only whole to the naked eye.
But I am a broken man my love
Would you still take me?

In a broken body I dwell
Struggling by the day
Praying by night
I am not a burden.

I will give you my life
Every shallow breath
Those that are deep come when I forget..
My hands
They would caress your face
Though they tremble to get there.
This broken body
I want you to have it.

The Best Portion of Your Life

We spend so long waiting
Waiting for those big moments:
To be married
For a child to be born
For success
The best portion of your life
Is none of these.
Those little moments spent smiling
Looking toward the sky
Grateful for everything.
Those little things
That simply take your breath away.

A Stranger in the Beginning

When you meet a stranger
Before your heart may reach out
It warns of a grave danger
If you do not listen, your heart may shout.

Pieces of your heart lie strewn about
Which piece would you give them?
The largest chunk?
A sure-fire way to drive 'em away.
A piece too small?
They cannot make something of nothing.
This I say to you…
Give them all of it
Pick up all the pieces…
With their cracks and all.
Give up your heart
For it is not so small.

Some strangers will seek to break it
A thousand pieces, broken into thousands more.
Instead, guard your heart
Though you give it freely.
Let your chest be of iron,
A flash so beautiful, cannot go undefended.

When you meet a stranger
Give them everything you have
They may need it more than you know.
But do not let them come as a thief
They cannot take more than you give
Stand guard around your heart.

Élyas Rivermark

A stranger may remain so
Yet a friend, they can become.
Even into a lover they could grow.
You may even end as you began.
Do not despair
You cannot control a stranger.

Put in all that you are
Hope for a bountiful return
Never hide a scar
Even when the bridges burn.
Know that you gave it your all
Sometimes strangers simply fall.

With Her

He was heartbroken and she was in love
Lonely but never alone
She was always on his mind
How could she be so kind?
Her beauty was beyond speech
She was in love
He was in despair
His hands with a constant tremble
A chest too short of breath
He was heartbroken, she was in love
He would never be
With Her

Élyas Rivermark

This Lament of the Heart

Through every season my heart weeps
In every moment it bounds and leaps
For in those little moments
Are the reasons that I must go on living
Let those minutes become a hundredfold
I wish to be happy
If I may be so bold
I know not what the future may hold
"It will get better"
So I am told.

I have changed so much since last we spoke
You did not find me before my heart broke.
Shattered to dust
A million pieces too small to give
Give them I must.
If only a gentle hand would take them
Some are crushed even smaller
This only adds to the fear.
Every day I give pieces of my broken heart
Forgive me if that does not seem very smart.
I know not how else to live…

Do not listen to this *lament of the heart*
I am a happy man.
Tormented by the strings of my heart.
It beats for so many
I would not have it any other way.

Hair Like the Harvest

Under a canopy of fire I lay
Leaves of red and gold falling.
I cannot think of anything more
But the girl with *hair like the harvest*
Shades of gold
Made bright by the eyes like a storm.
A smile that kills me
How I wish I knew her
This distance is too great
But her smile
That is enough…

Élyas Rivermark

Mercy

I may wear it, but this smile is false.
Each day passes like the last
A deep shadow descending further within me.
From flash to stone
Stone to iron
I no longer recognize my own heart
It lies in a darkness of its own making.
Too often does it fall
Never a hand to bring it back up.

Careless and pure it once was
Fit for the young chest it rested in.
I wish for that boy to return
Never have I seen such joy
One who's worries were so small.
That boy loved
He loved and cared so much
Year after year
That soft heart began to bleed,
Day after day tears flowed.

Now that heart has gone cold
Too many daggers have surrounded it.
That young chest
So pure and unblemished
Now riddled with scars.
What once put trust in others
Now gazes through jade eyes.
How they wish they would change
See the world as they once did…
With those rose-coloured eyes.

A Lament of the Heart

My eyes have changed, my heart has not
It is encased in iron
But it remains soft within
Reaching out, again and again.
Have *Mercy*
O Lord
Have *mercy* on this fragile heart
How often it breaks
How often do the thorns surround it
The scars bleed
Again and again.

With sorrow I place these words
For sorrow is all I know
Pain replaced joy
Tears for a smile
Misery is everything.
All this is hidden under a smile
A smile that has not changed.
One that favours the left side
Slightly crooked, seemingly genuine.
The boy became a man
Pushing everything down
Hiding from the world.

If you love this man
Have *mercy*
Mercy because he does not trust
He loves ever so dearly
But he is afraid
Will they leave one more scar?
Another knife in the back
When will the suffering end?

For until then
O Lord
Have *mercy* upon this broken man
Fill him with your love, with your peace
Let his heart be ready for her
Let it rejoice in your love.
This man loves you, more than he loves himself
He is lost
So please
Have *mercy*
Let me be patient
I await them that will love me, as I love you
I will chase them as I once was
A boy with stars in his eyes.
So
Until then
Have *mercy.*

Life on the Moon

In my heart I know it to be true
I do not belong here
Among the steel mountains
Rivers of asphalt roaring in my ears.
In the black of night
I gaze upon my true home
Up there among the stars.

They will never understand
My heart does not follow them
No creation of man may satisfy.
Where others find solace
I find pain and I am lost.
I am not like them.
I love too deep
My heart remains with them too long
They only ever see my shell.
Not the burning fire within.
A light so bright, it might be a star
I cannot let it out
Else it be devoured by them.

On this night, I gaze at the moon
It may be a dream
But I wish my life were there.
From the depths of my heart
I wish it were so.

Élyas Rivermark

In *life on the moon*
I would be free to love
As long as I desired to do so
The light burning within me
Would finally be reflected.
The legend of the man in the moon
I could make it true
For I would never be alone.

In those days I may hunt with Orion
Dance with the Sisters Seven
Go to war with Mars
Fall in love with Venus
Even find my way home with Sirius.
All this is *life on the moon*
How I wish it were so.

Yet here I am, living life on my own
A stranger to my own kind
They look at me in disgust
Proclaim the oddity before them.
I fear they do not know
The man in the moon walks with them.
So out of place but so bright
If only given the chance
I could shine for them.

My home is not here
No land on earth can satisfy
My home is on the moon
For only there I am normal
Only there I can shine so bright.
Every night I weep at the heavens
Banished now for so long
Every day I yearn for my old life
One of love and stars
My Life on the Moon

Élyas Rivermark

Feeling Alone in a Room Full of People

How does it feel to be lonesome?
Indeed, my mind aches when I am alone
But I do not wish to be in a room full of people.
For how could I bear the weight of their gaze?
I have often walked through this world
Lonesome, but not alone
Always surrounded by people
Never to escape the garden of my own making.

I imagine a stream, the creekbed of my dreams
Scenes of my life flow past without form.
I sit on a hill of green, listening to the memories flow.
I am reminded of life by the slow keys in my ear
Perhaps the quiet purr of a bow.
In the garden of my mind I have nothing to fear.

Do not dismay, my dear, I love this life
I simply wish to remain at peace
My mind is always restless, so full of strife
But the garden?
That is the place to which I may escape.
In the tumult of this world
I find I must escape more and more
Though I wish it were not so.
Now, I seem to find joy in being alone
Living through the cinema of my life
Often, I have found a smile on my face
Feeling alone in a room full of people.

No Thoughts

I see the snow fall, pillows of cotton growing on the ground
Tears welling up from the breaths of ice blowing.
There is no one, none living around
How I wish it would never stop snowing
Cover me in ice, let me sleep until spring shows its face.
My body is so warm, the cold cannot touch me
Under a blanket of white, my mind goes dim.

No thoughts

None at all

No Thoughts

It is better to live this way.
Too long has my mind wandered among the trees
Paths stretch out in twos and threes.
This snow has hidden the tracks of ancestors away
I know not which to take
So I do not think.
Simply wander through the forest.
Hoping to one day arrive at my home.
Arms to hold me
A fire to melt the ice from my eyes
Until that special day of freedom
I still wander through this life.
Following the shadow of a light before me.

No thoughts

None at all…

Élyas Rivermark

The Two Trees

In the East, there stood *the two trees*
One of life, one of death
One to give, one to take away my breath.
I wonder what kind they were
How I wish I could walk among those gardens.
To walk, surrounded by sheer beauty and grace.
Only in my dreams
Or perhaps, when my death takes me there.

In my dreams, I am transported there
Many trees and plants I do not know
Though *the two trees* in the distance
One so bright and blossoming
The other, so dark and enticing.
I want to see them
I want to see where man fell.
For the same blood runs in my veins, the same weakness.
Please Lord, in this moment, protect me,
Protect me from my blood of Adam.

As I walk through this garden,
I am reminded of the little things.
I see small animals scurrying about
Deer and aurochs grazing
Large animals basking in the sunlight.
In this place of my dreams
I am content
Listening to a song of birds.

A Lament of the Heart

At the glade of *the two trees*
I feel the presence of two spirits
That of Life.
Cherry blossoms flow through my mind
A wind of laughter and peace in their wake
I would eat of this tree everyday
Delighting in the creation that fills my heart.
In that moment, I felt a hand rest on my shoulder,
A font of vigour washed over me
The Lord was beside me, but I dare not look
For my blood called me to the other tree.

The tree of knowledge.
The bane of Adam called my name
A snake hung from its branches, sneering at my heart.
That of Death.
A world of disease, rot growing on the hearts of men.
I wish we had never eaten that fruit.
I wish we could have lived here with Him
But man is weak, if not for grace.
I wish to be in Heaven now
But my task in this world is not finished
So until my death, may it be far from me.
I will walk in this garden with Him
In my dreams, I am here
Standing in the glade of *the two trees*.

Not Kiss You

I have always wanted to change
Every night you are in my dreams
I have met you there.
How much I love you
How much I wish I could hold you
But I know that you do not want it
I know you know me not
You have only seen my face.
My words be taken by the wind
So at this moment…
The hardest thing in the world
How can I *not kiss you?*

A Forgotten Shade of Life

I have lived through many colours
The vibrant shades of my life begin to fade
Bright days of yellow and green
Have left me for shades of blue.
Indeed, there is not much left to do.
These rose-coloured eyes
Taken over by the strength of grey.
Like old photos, there is little life
Only a semblance of a second
Stuck forever in time.

In this life I am alone
Living in a world of grey and blue
Memories of times passed flow through my mind
Even the red of anger seems a comfort
How I wish I could return to that time before.
A life so bright and vibrant
Indeed

A forgotten shade of life…

Élyas Rivermark

Bandages

Pain in the body is a short sensation
The ache of a bullet
The fire of a blade
Those are as comfortable as old friends.
Scars abound upon my body
Their ache returns to me each morning
How easily they can be hidden
Under a soft blanket of *bandages.*

Where are they now?
There is not enough in this world
To soak up my tears.
In truth, each night I am afraid.
I have given my heart to many over the years
The loves I lost and the friends I made
I fear losing them.
My memories may never fade
For within my mind I may see them again.

So I ask not for *bandages*
Unlike wounds I do not wish to hide these
I show the world my heart with ease.
So many wounds and scars
Made by emotions uniquely ours.
As you trace these lines on my body
Would you also ask after my heart?
We never need *bandages*
For there is nothing wrong with a broken heart.

Every Key Was Pressed with Tears...

On fading footsteps I drifted
Down a path of dirt and leaves
Each step is more laborious than the last.
My body is broken
How closely it matches that in my chest.
I had believed that this forest could save
Pillars of wood like people in a crowd
Shadows to my eyes they drifted past.
Down this wooded path I limped
Calling out your name.
But You could not hear me.

I remember when my laments were quiet.
They came to me in the dead of night
Ghosts of my mistakes
Trying evermore to kill me.
Your touch made them quiet
Returning them to their graves
Clearing the garden of my mind.
Every weed is gone
Thorns now plucked from my hands.
All the harm once done to me
A faint memory.

My memories of you are beginning to fade
The hard ground crunching beneath me.
I see something in the glade ahead
It is something that is not supposed to be
Is it real, or just in my head?

Élyas Rivermark

This glen, it is so beautiful
Waves of green wash over me.
The faint smell of wood wafting
With ivory keys and black lacquer
A piano sat before me.
Begging to sing.

I wish I knew how to sing
To have my hands fly
Filling the air with melody and grace.
So I asked the piano:
"Would you teach me?"

Many nights passed, banging on the keys…
But they never made a sound.

As I lay in that meadow,
Listening to the songs of nature
Birds singing, deer crying
Crickets chirping, wolves howling.
I could not make sense of it.
Why will the piano not sing?

I remember your voice
The sweet tone with which you spoke.
To me, it was the perfect song.
Lullabies sung at night
Like our child I would drift
A slight smile on my face
In and out of sleep
Dreaming of the life we had made.
I miss you.
I miss you like the sun misses the flower.
You are no longer here

A Lament of the Heart

I have nothing to direct my love to.
I watch the piano now
I watch it and begin to say:

"It was a normal day
Though I wish we went the other way
Singing in the car as we always had.
The light was green like this glade
So I thought nothing more
Until another came on the right
Driving forward during a fight
Like paper crumpled in a bin
I could not blame them for their sin.
My world fell into black.
When I opened my eyes I was in a bed
A load of bandages around my head.
Alone in that room
No singing
Nor the laughter of a child
Months of blackened rain followed
Nothing to change my sorrow"

So I ask this once more
My piano in this forest
Would you sing with me?

Every key was pressed with tears,
But you could not hear me.

Élyas Rivermark

All of Us

Sometimes, I do not like my own heart
Even after two years apart
She attacks my name.
All of us, we are not the same.
These men who came after me
They hurt you with who they claimed to be.
Each one of them, seeming worse than the last
I wish you would stop saying *all of us.*
I was not like them.
I truly loved you in our past.

To all the men
You said we lied, your letters said otherwise.
I used to keep them
I kept them for a year
Hoping that maybe something would change.
My heart remained yours for too long
So before you say *all of us* are the same.
Remember my letters
How I called your name.

The Sixth Language

Dearest Beloved,

I am sure you have heard of the five famous languages of love. To be truthful, I do not believe they are complete. There is a language missing, or perhaps, it is the language that birthed the other five. All my life, I have thought about which of the five suits me best. They each have their own merits and I am blessed when I am shown all of them.

The language of touch. It depends entirely on from whom the touch comes. Truly, I enjoy a hug from time to time, I desire some form of physical contact, but not for too long. It must only last as long as I feel it is right. Nor do I really enjoy it when it comes as a surprise, unless of course it comes from you. When I think of you, I would have you touch me as often as you were willing. This does not mean sex, no, for me, it is much more complex. I want to feel the touch of your fingers through my hair as we watch our favourite television show. Your arm to hook through mine as we walk down the pavement. The sweet caress of you with a small pat of reassurance on my back. I want to rest my hand on your thigh as we talk through a long trip on the road. A small kiss on my cheek as you pass by while I am writing. Indeed, the intimacy of sex means nothing if everything that comes before it is not there.

The second language, that of affirmation. Words that bring praise and life-giving speech. I do not care much for this idea. Words of praise often make me feel insincere in my gratitude. Too much awkwardness comes from my response. I also care very little for the praise of others, as I often discredit the sincerity of their words. As you can glean from my words, I care very much for the sincerity of myself and of others. I do not want to hear that I am a good writer, a good chef, or even that I am a good person. There is so much more sincerity in telling a person how something makes you feel. I want to know how you connected to my poems, the echoes that sounded in your heart. Tell me what you hated, what made you fume, hold nothing back for I must know every corner of you. I feel more of your love if there is critique in your praise. I am blessed to be gifted in some skills which have earned some earnest compliments. They are always wondrous to hear but I will also thrive and grow if I am made aware of my wrongdoings.

Gifts, gifts are perhaps one of my favourite things. Though not because I am a material man, rather it is a product of the sixth. It is not the "what" that matters to me, it is the reason why. My darling if you were to give me a rock because it made you think of me, then my face would surely light up. An expensive watch means nothing, a car is the same, the higher the price the less likely I am to enjoy it. I am reminded of a couple birthdays of mine. My grandma bought me a dutch oven one year. I had been talking about making stews, chowders and even experimenting with no-knead bread for the winter. She bought me the oven and even printed a recipe for the bread and put it in the box. Years earlier, a friend of mine gave me a small plastic keychain of a VW Beetle to put on my key rings for the very same car. What sets these kinds of gifts apart is that both my friend and my grandma listened to me and knew me well enough as a person to get something that would bring me much joy. The best kind of gift are those that are not on the list. At all times I try to be vigilant and listen for the ideas for gifts that often go unspoken, small comments that go unnoticed. This is the type of love that really shows.

The fourth language becomes so important later in life. In marriage and in love we ought to live in service to one another. I struggle with accepting this form of love from anyone. It feels strange to say this, but this language often makes me feel incompetent. From work, to writing, to other things, my constant state of busyness overthrows some of the tasks I must do. Things are left uncleaned, broken things remain slightly too long and some bonds suffer for it. To have someone offer to do these for me is truly a blessing and I am always appreciative. I must tell you that I am learning how to respond better to this language. There are some that come naturally to us, but all of these languages can be learned. I am discovering this by the day.

The last language is the most important, from it comes the other four. Those who do not enjoy this are strange to me. How can you profess to love someone if you do not give them your undivided attention when they need it most? If there is no time spent with you, unplugged from this world, our love will not grow, I may not touch you, I cannot praise the ways in which you have blessed me. I cannot discover clues for the small gifts I wish to give you. How will I hear what small services I can alleviate from your life? If I spend little to no time with only you, how can I love you?

Out of one idea these languages of love flow so strongly. The language I have added, the sixth language, is the language of effort. Effort and constant pursuit. I have often heard that love should be 50/50, I believe this is an unfair assessment. Love should be 60/40, both you and I, striving to be 60. I mean this not as a competition, but rather both you and I put forth maximum effort at all times. Each day I will try to give a little bit extra of myself. Even if I do not have that much more to give, to you I will still give it. With the effort of constant pursuit also comes the increased need for constant communication, new ways to learn more about each other's hearts. I must be truthful and say that this language has never been returned to me except from my family and from God. In this shallow world around me, I believe that so many have been lied to. They have been told that too much effort leads to heartbreak. I ask them: "So what?"

Élyas Rivermark

I have said this many times: a thousand times I would bleed, a thousand times I would break. If this means that each drop of blood and each time my heart breaks it brought me one step closer to finding you, then I would suffer for as long as it takes to be led to you. To each person in my life, I will pour in my full effort, in hopes that one day it will be you who returns my heart to me. Indeed, I grow weary of the cycle, it is so difficult to hold my heart out, praying it will not be burned. I pray this cycle will end soon, my efforts to find you do not seem to be working, you are hidden from me. In this sea of faces I cannot find you. My darling, please, please come and save me, end this vicious cycle.

I will always be

The Knight of Your Heart

Élyas

Just For a Moment Everything Felt Still

With my head resting on soft moss
The wind gently singing over the cliffs
Leaves dancing and twirling in the sky
I can hear the call of the ocean in the distance.
Waves breaking on a grey coast
I closed my eyes.
The scratch of wool on my back
Felt similar to the beard on my face.
I paid them no mind
For it began to wander elsewhere.

Naturally I thought of you
Though the tumult that used to come
Now reduced to a pondering feeling.
Just for a moment everything felt still
My heart was at peace.
Your face flashed before me, as it often did
Our life is stretching out in my mind.
Be at peace, He has said to me
She will come
That is enough for me.
So I wait, listening to the Earth speak.

A pillow of moss for my head
I lie there listening…
A piano began to play in my head.
The keys humming a beautiful melody
It was not happy, nor full of sorrow
It was as all things
Fitting the moment of today, not tomorrow
Meant for peaceful moments.

Élyas Rivermark

The piano brought a smile to my lips
In my minds eye I could see the trees
They towered behind me.
Singing a song of their own
Wood creaking and groaning
A choir unlike any other
Their voices are sombre and inviting.
As the wind blew through their leaves
I thought I heard the whistle of flutes
Prancing through the air.
Alone on those cliffs, I never felt lonely
Only at peace.

Just for a moment everything felt still
I wish I could spend an eternity there
Sleeping on Earth's bed
Listening to her sing.

Tired of Trying to be Stronger than I Feel

So often they ask how I am
In truth I am doing everything I can.
Slowly, I am fading away
Each day passes as the rest
Each motion is done out of instinct.
It grieves me to see myself in this state
I do not know how to escape these shackles.
Tired of trying to be stronger than I feel

I am a man
Unable to divulge my emotions
Without respect, how will I live?
I cannot heed the lies I am told
To let my emotions fly.
Women do not truly understand them
Nor do I want to be a boy in her eyes.
Other men are my refuge
But truly, they feel the same as I.
We have enough burdens to bear
Doomed to suffer alone.
Modernity has failed us
Shadows of men now wander the streets
Fighting their demons without reprieve.

We grow weary in this century
Never finding love
Shying away from its hypocrisy.
Men are desperate for a gentle touch
Perhaps a promise of eternal love.
Instead, this world is in delusion
A bare minimum shifts ever upward.

Élyas Rivermark

Without form, we cannot reach it.
Even if we do, we are betrayed.
Men are leaving the pool
Leaving only dirt and vile.
Like lights in a storm
We are gradually being snuffed out.

"There are no good, honest men"

We are here, in the quiet, in the shadows
Tired of trying to be stronger than we feel.

I believe we have heard it all:
Men are a source of currency, nothing more
A source of pleasure
Our bodies in war
Muscle with no intellect
Made to make a home in the garbage
Nothing more…
A man's heart is not made for this modern love
Every knight desires a princess
To one day make a queen.
We do not believe you are weak
Only that we would have someone to die for
To cherish and admire
Would you let us do it?

This world has killed us
We do not teach men to be men.
Now, a twisted form rules
Vile, lustful and small.
Like goblins they dirty the beautiful things
Always greedy for more.
Like knights, good men must kill them

Throw off their disguise.

We must wait, watch them plunder
Real men are hated.
Our strength is ridiculed, set in chains
Told we are worth nothing.
Now they search for us
No longer blinded by hypocrisy
Where are we?
In the shadows, in the quiet
Tired of trying to be stronger than we feel.

Lost Without You

A path through the darkness
Each step I cannot see
Only the sweet touch of your hand.
Sweet words and kindness
I never wonder where you may be
With you I may stand
My head held high
Without a light in the sky
I would wander through life
Lost without you.

You Don't Have to Pretend Anymore

I hear your cries
When all of the world is against you
Look to the skies
For that is the only thing to do.

Your heart is beautiful to me
Your voice comes bounding over the hills.
In it are the pains of sorrow
Years of ache and failed speech
They hide so that I may not see
But my beloved you are known to me.
You don't have to pretend anymore.

For every tear that you have shed
I will give you joy when we are wed.
Every fit of anger
Emotions deemed fit to hide
Bring them out to me and lament.
With my left under your head
My right in a tight embrace
Listen to my voice.
It comes leaping upon mountains
Skipping upon hills
Rise up and come away
For your winter is dead and gone.
I have grown flowers for you
Like honey my lips wait for you
Our love will blossom like spring.

Élyas Rivermark

I ask that you forget your winter
Let your heart forgive itself
Do not pretend for my sake.
There are scars and pains
Let them out.
I will still hold you
My body is yours
Let it shield you from the arrows
The flame that comes to consume
You don't have to pretend anymore.

I know the ones who have lied.
Hear this truth now:
You are an oasis for my soul
From a desert I escaped
Burning fire always beneath me
My heart blackened by them.
My love
You saved me, gave me water
Like clay under the sun, I am cracked.
I became shapeable once more.
So form me into something new.
Be it a sword or shield
I will protect you from them.
Into a cup that you may drink
You saved me once.
May it be that I will do the same?

I Wish You Weren't So Far Away

They say distance makes the heart grow fonder
When I think of you I cannot help but wander
Into the garden of my mind
Where you are so gentle and so kind.
An angel and a saint
When I see you I feel faint.
Please turn away from me
Your eyes see who I am
And who I am meant to be.
You have left me in the desert bare
Without your love, I do not care.
I would travel the stars
Across oceans and the lands between
Just to see you once more
So in love and so lost
I will see you no matter the cost
I wish you weren't so far away.

You have gone where I cannot follow
Indeed, I feel so hollow
Your beauty I can no longer see
Some years ago, you were gone from me.

Élyas Rivermark

In sorrow I write these lines
Though you are bright as the sun shines.
On wings of light you fly
Above every mountain and every river
Blessing us who yet remain below.
An angel you were on Earth
So it remains.
Forever beautiful, too much to show
Forever I will love you.
I wish you weren't so far away.

As the rain falls, I remember it
I love and hate the memory
For it was the last time I saw you
The morning after
You had something to do.
Looking back, I should have gone
Maybe I could have stopped them
I could have flown in your place
With wings of light like yours
It would be me, up in the sky.

Wine touched our lips
The gentle purr of music in our ears
Everything in black, white, and brown.
You were truly beautiful that night
Your hair fell in ringlets down your back
Eyes like doves
They saw through me to my core.
Lips like honey, I remember their touch
Curving slightly
Like you knew something I did not.
From it rang a laugh, pure as crystal
How I wish to hear it once more.

A Lament of the Heart

A dark green dress
You knew it was my favourite
It teased things I had never seen
Only marriage could unlock those secrets.

We talked into the night
Now I know the time was right.
The ring, it was in my pocket
Waiting to come forth
Once we were alone that night
Dancing in the dark.

You were to leave in the morning
Some place far away
But I did not know it.
We walked that night
Over bridges and streets, hands together.
Not long left to travel.
On that bridge
Slow dancing before the end
You leaned in close to me.
Assaulted by the smell of cinnamon and wine
I could not resist much longer.
The ring appeared before your eyes
Glittering in the starlight.
I asked you then
Would you be with me?

My bride to be,
How beautiful was she
Those kisses were better than any
I knew there were to be many.

Élyas Rivermark

I left you that night,
Now I know I should have stayed
For in the morning, we were betrayed
I wish you weren't so far away.

A morning full of confusion and panic
Of it I remember nothing
It is too painful to bear.
Only a call
That was all
They said you were gone
On wings of white
Flying high in the sky.
I often ask God why
Why must you have been taken from me?
Now only memories of green remain
The smell of wine and cinnamon
A slow dance in the dark.
They are all I keep of you
Everything else brings pain.

If I could ask God one thing
It would have been to stop the moon
Stop the moon
Make that night last a lifetime.
Your smile and laughter forever, how it ought to be.
I know I will see you soon
I will tell you of my life
Though I know you are here
Sometimes I feel you in my strife
Touching my face as you once did
A smile that knows what I do not.

A Lament of the Heart

My love,

I wish to hold you again
I wish to kiss your lips
I wish to marry you
I wish I could have kept my promise
I wish to love you…

I wish you weren't so far away.

Élyas Rivermark

You Don't Have To Say You Are Okay

Fifteen minutes
A time that seems so short
Can feel like an eternity
Full of joy feels like but a second
Sleeping, even less
A song of that length is not heard
Though its quality is in the stars.
Fifteen minutes of tears
Those may be the longest.
Years, months, days all together
Felt in so short a time.
Listen to me now
You don't have to say you are okay.

My love
To those that hurt you
Shed no tears for them.
It is not your fault
It is **not** your fault
It is not **your** fault
Like goblins in the night
They sought to steal what shined.
Your heart like gold
Covered in dirt and grime.
I pray you find one to wash it clean
Bring it back to life.

A Lament of the Heart

Though you cry every day
Know that there are those that love you
Alas, I know you not
For you I would be shot.
Dead in your place if I am able
Those like me, they are no fable
Behind that horde of filth
Gleaming they stand
Their hands outstretched.

The love you are searching for
From him and family it ought to come
Became twisted
Found in the form of acts and contracts.
My love
True love is not this way
It crosses mountains
Storms cannot hold it back.

From wind do the trees bend and sway
Love is a fortress
Made from the strongest foundation
You don't have to say you are okay
Only come and find rest
You and me, we can only do our best.

My love you have much strength
Eyes that could kill
A brow raised at the sight of lies.
I can only dream of such skill
You do not have to be okay
It seems we never are
Our bodies, always at war
Doomed to fight our minds forever.

Élyas Rivermark

Day by day
Minute by minute
Our life falters on
In joy we laugh and in sorrow we cry
Anger always seems to have its place.

Up hills and down
This life ponders on
So please
Take a moment and look
Do you see?
You don't have to say you are okay
Neither are we
It is not our fault
Only one star in all of the sky
We each shine with our own light
Please do not cry
If you do…

You don't have to say you are okay

Such a Simple Thing

I awoke one morning
To *such a simple thing*
From the horrid landscape of my dreams
To the most beautiful, most wondrous scene.
This life I have been given
Images of you flow through my mind.
I thought I knew about love
In this quarter of a century
This scene tells me I truly know nothing.

My eyes turned toward you
Brushing your teeth in the morning.
The horrors of the night now banished
I watched you there before me
Wearing only my t-shirt
Looking like a beautiful mess.
Hold me in the darkness
Forgive my restlessness.
You looked at me…
Toothbrush in hand, hand on your hip.

"What"

I smiled
Nothing, Nothing at all
Such a simple thing

Élyas Rivermark

Waking from a Dream

Light burned through the early morning mist
No alarm, even the cat slumbered on.
I did not wake
Plagued by dreams unfit for sleep.
I could not wake
Each night as the phases of the moon passed
My unconscious mind played many films
Strapped hands and feet, I could not escape.

Demons attacked each night
With them came images I wish I could unsee.

A man with a gun before me
He wore a mask
That of a face I did not recognize.
I stood before him, unable to move, unable to speak
I wished only to move my eyes from this scene.
Frantically climb from this Hell.
Yet I slumbered on.
My family kneel before me
So too my friends
One by one the shots rang through my mind
An ever growing pool of blood surrounded my feet.
Sweating, light entered my eyes
Small green eyes stared at me from above.
What a dreadful way to start a morning.
Waking from a dream.

A Love Idea

I ponder and I wait
Alone, but never far away
Always wondering what to do.
By now I have accepted my fate
A solitary life down by the bay
The world escapes with the morning dew.
Peace as the waves crash.
The image of you fading away
A love idea
Too far now to catch.

Élyas Rivermark

The Break of Dawn

'Tis so quiet in the dead of night
Away from the veins of asphalt
Monsters roaring with all their might.
The constant purr of the roads
Broken by horns and sirens
Nothing quiet until the light.
How wonderful to be away from it all
In a house made from the souls around
The smell of sap and moss ever present.
In this place it is hard not to fall
To fall into the silence of little sound.

At the first glimpse of light
The forest may awaken
Beautiful sounds so unlike the city
They change through the seasons.

In a landscape covered in ice
The sound is the silence
Water that no longer moves
A soft blanket of white covers the ground.
It is the silent nature of silence:
深々[1]
しんしんしんしん[2]
Snow is falling
For we all know its sound.

---

[1] "Shinshin" - Japanese onomatopoeia used to describe the sound of snow falling silently; "a sound with no sound"
[2] Hiragana form of shinshin

A Lament of the Heart

When the flowers bloom
So too do the sounds
At *the break of dawn.*
A symphony of voices ring across the trees
Small streams lift up their gurgle
Birds sing in the morning light
Lifted to my ears by the wind
Rustling leaves and blossoms from the their perch
Though the silence has fled
Music has returned to my heart
Exalting the spirit within.

Earlier and earlier the light comes
Bringing heat and danger along with it
New voices are among those from before.
One, maybe two more
Insects begin to buzz
Frogs that grunt like a drum.
From symphony to cacophony
The call of the wild becomes so loud
Much too soon at *the break of dawn*
The city and the forest are much the same.
Though the latter much easier to bear
I am grateful for the change
As there is much to be done.

The heat begins to recede
Forests of fire return to the Earth
Every breath used for preparation
Everything seems hard at work.
In anticipation
Anticipation of the coming silence.

Élyas Rivermark

How beautiful and terrible is this time
I must say that it is my favourite.
More sleep
A gentle kiss of ice on the wind.
Here I am wrapped in flannel and denim
Listening to the symphony reach a resolution.
Like any great story
So too must this one come to an end.
Only to return once more
Every year
At *the break of dawn.*

A Shepherd in His Field

In the fields of green I slept
Wildflowers grew beneath my feet
Their scent ever present in my nose
In that field I sat, I wept.

In my mind came a sea of faces
Pieces of my heart I had given to all
With soft words and a tender touch
I led them to the beauty of the field
Away from their home; beyond the wall.
Truly I tell you, I love them all too much
Each day I spend with them
So many details…
I wish to listen forever
For their stories are music to my ears.
A window to my heart
I could not bear to lose but one.

O Lord, to lose that which I love
One face that has turned away
Yet, the rest continue their stories.
May I leave them?
My soul reaches out to that who is lost
Their story was my favourite…
The way their eyes glinted
A smile whispered when they spoke
Hands speaking more than the mouth.
Always with rapture I listened to them.

Élyas Rivermark

Father, I must leave now
To return that which was lost.
Back to greener pastures
A crown of daisies upon their brow.
We would treat them as if they had never left.
Listening to their story once more with joy.
How I want to see those stars again
Dancing in their eyes when they spoke
To be entranced by their words
A smile on my face once more.

Lord
You have made me *a shepherd in this field.*
A pasture of the deepest green
Wildflowers ever under my feet
My spirit reaches to those who are lost
From their home and beyond the wall.
To listen to their stories
To laugh and to cry with them
Day by day
I have invited you to come
In this sea of faces…
I see how yours lights up
A shepherd to his sheep
I will always come back for you.

The First Blink of Sunshine

A ray of light falls like gossamer from the sky
Sown from God's hand.
Drawn closed are the Ides of March
Leaving a cold and dreary landscape behind.
Winter has its own beauty
A bright white landscape stretches
Little mirrors falling from the eaves
It is truly a wonder to see.
Webs of branches
Pillars of brown and white
All under a shadow of snow capped peaks.

But

The first blink of sunshine
Splashes of colour in a blank wasteland
How the warmth seems to seep down
All sense of loss flees its touch.
The sun smiles upon the Earth
Promising so much.
What a joy to be outside.

Sunshine brings so much to life
Even through pain
There is something about the first sunburn.
A late-night rush to the drug store
Aloe Vera and Aquaphor.
After the bonfires and never before
Steamed like a lobster of the same colour
A post-sun nap and nothing more.

Élyas Rivermark

With the promise of longer days
Thoughts of fruits and flowers abound in my head
How I love the berries
Rhubarb pies and watermelon slices
Chips and salsa by the pool
Maybe a margarita or two.
The first blink of sunshine
All these bright memories come flooding back.
They push away the gloom
Bring a smile to my face
Thank God for warmer weather
I cannot wait
For the world to bloom.

Baking Cookies

Notes of vanilla
Under shear clouds of flour
They fall upon me like pollen in the spring
How much I want to inhale
Let the warmth of it engulf me
Only to sneeze; such a silly thing.

It begins as it often does
With butter and sugar
Granulated or brown it does not matter
A slight crunch
The taste of home, light with the first
With brown it is something different.
Like caramel and almonds on your tongue
A fuller flavour for everyone.

The mixture becomes fluffy
A colour like the beach,
A texture to match,
An egg or two to bind it together
Or so it ceases to be.

The most important comes next.
Vanilla bean or its essence
Either one provides the necessary presence.
Sweet smells fill the kitchen
A few ingredients left I would say
Closer to keeping the sadness at bay.

Élyas Rivermark

Flour, soda and salt
They form such a perfect dough
Full of memories
Moments lost within the past
Only one left to go.

Chocolate, sweet chocolate
Without it these are nothing
Morsels that melt and stretch.
From little balls of dough
Comes the essential piece of the night
To be shared
Soaking up milk as we speak.
I tell you there is nothing better
Than *baking cookies.*

Cherry Blossoms (さくら)

Like rivers of pink through the branches
They ebb and flow like the tide
Without words they speak to me
Even as they fall
A ballet of flowers before my eyes
They spell out the word:

さ
く
ら
[3]

Oh how they fall
Dancing in the wind like snow
Transporting all those who see
Into the most beautiful fantasy.

Have you seen them?
桜の花 [4]
They blossom but once
Covering everything in a warm glow
Just as the birds begin to chirp
The insects begin to buzz
Each time I see them
Deeper in love do I fall
A promise of new life
An extension of my own soul.

---

[3] Sakura
[4] "Sakura no hana" - Sakura Blossoms

Élyas Rivermark

I go there in my mind
To the place where they go
東京 [5]
On the outskirts of the city
Places raided with pink
Perhaps images of blood and snow
Middling within.
Even so, the sky becomes vibrant
Even now the wind has a pen.
It writes so many things
But only for those with the eyes to see.
Songs it has written
Stories it wants to tell
And yet
Only for so short a time.
These *cherry blossoms* tell their own:

悲しみにさようなら [6]

---

[5] Tōkyō
[6] "Kanashimi ni sayōnara" - Goodbye to sadness

A River Runs Through It

I have spoken of the garden
It blooms forever in my mind.
Full of flowers and green pastures
Even the darker things
They hide in the corners
Beneath the shade of the cherry trees.
A river runs through it.
How I love its sound
Eroding dirt and grime.
Cleansing water rushes through me
Letting only beauty remain.

Élyas Rivermark

For When You Are Alone

I know how much it hurts
The flames seem to edge closer
The walls that you had once built
Long have they been dust.
Leaving a soft heart exposed
O how it yearns for a glance
The soft touch of a gentle hand
I need only a moment
Would you listen?

Do you hear the grace of my hands?
How they dance across the keys.
A sad melody fills the air
It is *for when you are alone.*
Let my hands sing to you
Like the songbirds in the night
Let my voice wash over you.
See how my eyes gaze upon your face.

I have reduced my walls to nothing
My only defence is this:
Polished wood and ivory keys
My voice has vanished
For my hands have a much stronger voice.
For when you are alone
Maybe you will hear me.

Come Home With Me

Into the entrance of my home
Your decorations line the walls
Your clothes cover the floor
The taste of your lips like honeycomb
Fresh, as I roam these halls.
The spirit of you, whom I adore
You are already here,
I must overcome this fear.
It is now our home
Never only mine
Come home with me.

Élyas Rivermark

Cradled in Your Arms

I do not remember those times
Held in the arms of my mother and father.
From the moment my mind came to me.
I remember the busyness
Hustling and bustling around all my life
Never once have I stopped.
From sports to school, to friends and girls
My heart sped along this path of life
Every second flashing like a mist
Even now I feel myself slipping
Sliding down this hill, going ever faster.
Can nothing slow me down?

How I wished to be older
That time has come.
How I wish I was younger
Spring has come and gone.
I budded and blossomed
My leaves stretch far into the open sky.
Such a great strength flows from me.
Great weights can be lifted off of my shoulders.
Indeed, there is the beginning of a philosopher's mind.
Musings rampage through my mind
Day and night I cannot rest.
Time I do not have
Never enough in a day.

A Lament of the Heart

O, to be in my mother and father's arms again
A time when I knew nothing
No sorrow, no joy
Nothing my conscious mind could comprehend.
Only the means to survive
A love that is still with me now.
My heart guards against it
My hands push the cradle away.
I have grown up
I no longer need a cradle of arms
My strength alone is enough.

How the devil comes for me
The Prince of Darkness comes
Tearing my heart from me
Wounding my hands
Piercing a gentle heart.
I am dead.
To be cradled in Your arms again
Lord, raise me up, kiss my brow.
I do not know how to live
Show me how.
My strength alone is never enough.

I have become naked
Not cradled in arms
Armour of muscle gone from me.
For it cannot defend against those weapons
Weapons that pierce not the body
But the soul is left wounded.

Élyas Rivermark

I walk behind my Father
Heavenly strength pours from him
Burning every demon that comes for me.
Sometimes I stray from His shadow
Only to return bleeding
Heartbroken once more.

My darling, do you know this feeling?
To have struggled so long
Scars and wounds abound on my skin
Though you cannot see them.
Cradled in His arms
They disappear
One by one
My mistakes always replace them.
That which was healed, returns burned
Why must I continue to do evil against myself?

I cannot seem to slow my life
Days like hours, like minutes, like seconds.
My dear, how do I slow it down?
My God keeps pace with me
Running when I know I should walk.
Cradled in His arms I could walk.
Through the valley
Slowly bearing the weight of the shadow of death.
Cradled in your arms
I would stop
A cord of three shows more strength.
My world would freeze as the minutes rushed by.
Trapped in time by the light of your eyes.
A new set of arms around me
Our strength will always be enough.

From 辛い to 幸せ[7]

A thousand times I would bleed
A thousand times I would break.
Words that escape my mouth
How often I say them to myself
So little to keep me going.
My fate in this world is doom
Such a small step could change this gloom
Off my rough path, onto one well beaten.
How slim and narrow it is
But on it are the articles of life.
Great lights shine on this dirt
The shadow of doom long dissipated.

辛い
A word to describe the shadows of my past
Behind them are pains that will last.
Bitterness seems to flow from my heart.
Heartbreak sits so proudly in my mind.
I am stuck in this prison
One of my own making.
I have the key to my release
But indeed, the Hell that awaits
Terrifies me more than the one I know.
Only one line, one step away could change me.

[7] 辛い (Tsurai) - painful, bitter, heart-breaking
幸せ (Shiawase) - happiness, good-fortune, luck, blessing

Élyas Rivermark

辛い
How I wish I could say goodbye
I have become comfortable in it
Painful, bitter, heart-breaking
A life such as this is all I know.
Clouds cover my days
Evil comes for my dreams in the night.
No rest
Only a pain I cannot escape.
One line, one step
It could all change in a word.

幸せ
This fit of fate is good.
A state of happiness that is new to me.
To be put together
To fit in this world created for me.
Indeed, I am blessed
Blessed to live this life.
Even through all the tears and pain,
I find myself clinging to life.
I see its light in every corner
Beauty abounds in this world
With the light of day I see it.
I cannot help but smile.

幸せ
Such a small change,
One step makes the biggest difference.
From clouds and terror
To sunlight and joy.
I walked in the darkest valley for too long.
I am lucky to have stepped into the light.

幸せ太り[8]
To put on weight from the good life.
How thin my life had become
For sorrow and anger cannot satisfy.
Full of faith and joy
I feel fuller than any other day in my life.
How blessed I have become.

To the stars
Without pain in my life
That is how far I may love.
To share my life
From 辛い to 幸せ
I will keep the darkness at bay.
From the Hell I know
To an unknown so vast
I will take my first step.
One line to make all the difference
I will embrace my life
Let it hold me until I die.

[8] 幸せ太り (しあわせぶとり, shiawasebutori) - putting on weight from the good life.

Élyas Rivermark

When I Dream of You

Month after month
I have been plagued by nightmares.
Afraid to sleep, afraid to lie awake
Visions are always in my head.
They bring forth every evil emotion under the sun.
Anger spills over
Hatred oozes from the deepest cracks in my heart
Jealousy and envy are hot within me
How I loathe their touch.
The night spews images I never want to see:
My family dead at my feet
Friends shot while I cannot look away
Wounds abound on my body
Past loves come back to haunt me.
Would the Lord release me from this agony?

I am allowed a brief respite
One or two nights,
No horror, no gore
Only strange stories in my head
Those that have no sense
They leave me feeling quite dense.
Full of anxiety for the day ahead.

I have tried many remedies
The tart juice of cherries
Powdered magnesium compounds
Roots of different kinds.
The only thing left is earnest prayer.
Take away the horrors

A Lament of the Heart

Let peace be in my mind once again.
Visions of beauty,
Images to match the world around me.

It is so seldom now
When I dream of you
I am at the bottom of a long path
Up the mountain.
Step by laborious step
I am climbing these stairs of my life.
Never two at a time,
One step
And another
I cannot seem to go any faster.

When I dream of you
I know that I am almost finished
Your touch will banish all other dreams
I may once again focus my eyes on beauty
Emotions of joy, peace and faith may return to me.
Until then I may suffer
Day and night
My waking nightmare rages
But *when I dream of you*
I may sleep once more.

Élyas Rivermark

The Girl with the Book

Confined to a corporate prison
Often do I walk the streets of the city
To let the sun and the wind touch my skin
I see the beauty of this world collapse
Surround my soul.
I have glasses to shield my eyes
To dull the brightness of their grey hue.
I may also walk and watch
See those living their lives alongside mine
I wonder what they are thinking
Do they feel rapture in the sun as I do?

I do not often think as I walk
Music drones in my ear
A sort of soundtrack for my own film.
Walking down these streets,
Straightbacked and expressionless
I wonder what they are thinking
Who do they see when I walk by?

What feels like the infinite time
I went for a walk to escape my desk
The smell of stale air and fluorescence
A small adventure to break up the day.
It began as it often did
The song of the wind in the leaves
Monsters driving past.

Across the first street and into the city
Into the food district.
Those feasting on the delicacies of the world.

The smell of coffee wafting
Grilled meats and fried foods
One street held it all
Doors to another world of food
How I love all that this street holds.
Through and past it always,
A fresh scent so opposed to my beige home.

My eyes never rest.
From one scene to the next
I am always watching those around me
Never with judgement or malice
Only a curiosity
To gain a brief glimpse into another life.
Those walking with their dogs
Friends eating by the way
Businessmen and politicians hustling through
Every so often
The most beautiful girl in the world.
I am struck dumb
Never to see her again.
All their shadows flow past
Holding onto the stress of the day.

The girl with the book
I did not expect to see one like her.
Her shadow was utterly different.
A strange feeling
She outshined even her shadow.
I was walking by the way
Watching the world.
Indeed, it seems she was in her own.
She sat in front of me on a bench
Absorbed in a page of a new world

Élyas Rivermark

Perhaps not one dissimilar to our own.
I did not intend it, my steps slowed
The music in my ear grew quiet
As I edged closer, she shined brighter.
She rose from her seat
Throwing a glance toward me,
What beauty!
Tall and slender,
She was draped in black, caressed in flowers
Dark ravens flowed down her back
Everything about her was dark
Though the light shone from within.
Once more I was struck dumb
Cursed to continue walking.
She passed into a store full of stars,
Where only angels may work
The girl with the book
May I ever see her again?

Finally at Peace

Here at the end of all things
At once I find it strange
To lie here
Staring up at the stars
Each one holds a story
Some sad, some full of glory.
What is my life?
So full of joy, pain and strife
I cannot help but love it
Not entirely good, nor wholly bad
It is the only one I have ever had
I love my life
Every little moment, created for me.

I remember how it smelled
The dirt diamond that dominated my youth
I once believed it held my future
To become a man much like Babe Ruth.
My life was not there
Over time I could not care.
Looking back now, I wish I could return there.

From a diamond to a page
I too became something else.
The smell of paper and musk
How I found profound comfort in it.
Alas, that also began to fade as the dusk.
In the fields of green and fresh grass
To perfumes and freshly painted nails
Full of sport and women my memories were
All I could think about was her.

Élyas Rivermark

Dreams of politics
Entering a world unlike my own
My mind flowed through life
Shifting from one comfort to the next
Waiting on a call, on a text.
Drinking one too many an ale
Seeking women, pretty and pale.
Forgive me these words
They fly and shift like birds
Here is the truth now
Finding peace, I knew not how.

Throughout this life
I thought peace could be found on Earth.
In meditation my mind fell blank
Falling into neverending nothing
A void that swallowed me whole.
In it I found nothing
Nothing at all
Peace is not nothing
Nor the absence of thought
It is so much more.

Is there peace in drink?
Full of wine I have no cares
Evil thoughts flee my mind.
But too much drink
Those thoughts return once more
Stronger and worse than before.

A Lament of the Heart

There is peace in true love
It does not appear until it is true
I ran to many women
In their bosom I found rest.
My true love has fled from me
For I am not worthy of her.
She will have peace
To her I must bring my own.

Who has peace?
Those loving a grateful life
Full of faithfulness, enduring faithfulness
Courage in the eyes of evil
Strength in the ability to forgive.
Allowing a past to fade
In those things there is peace
A place to rest in the shade.

I have learned this
Many years it takes
In this wind and rain
My heart raises a shout of joy.
Finally at peace
I am ready to find you
In true love I will keep you.

Would you wait for me?

A Letter at the End of It All

Dearest Beloved,

Here at the end of all things, I believe I have become stronger and better than I was. I know now how to love you according to your own heart. I did not always know, my love was feeble long ago, full of holes and false faces.

Here and now, I have very little to say, you have read the words that were tattooed on my heart. The emotions that flowed from me like a river of blood. I cannot hide from you how I feel, I cannot hide behind these walls I have built, for now you are inside. Stay close to my heart and I will care for you more than your heart can bear. My love for you will overflow, a flood of kisses and sweet words will always follow.

Do not be far from me and I will always be…

The Knight of Your Heart

Élyas

www.ingramcontent.com/pod-product-compliance
Lightning Source LLC
Chambersburg PA
CBHW051724040426
42447CB00008B/959
9798988814306